Rhoda Le

ELSA WAS BORN A DOG,

I WAS BORN A HUMAN ...

THINGS HAVE CHANGED

Rhoda Lerman

BLUE HEAVEN PUBLISHING
PORT CRANE, NY

ELSA WAS BORN A DOG, I WAS BORN A HUMAN ... THINGS HAVE CHANGED

For information, email: bobrhoda@aol.com or visit: www.blueheavenbooks.com

ISBN: 978-0-9892793-1-4

Cover illustration: *The Last of the Litter,* originally published by the Wilson Chemical Co.

Cover Design: Susan Rankin

ALSO BY RHODA LERMAN

In The Company Of Newfies

Animal Acts

God's Ear

The Book Of The Night

Eleanor

The Girl That He Marries

Call Me Ishtar

For our Molly whose molecules keep rearranging themselves into the most remarkable of dogs, generation after generation

ELSA WAS BORN A DOG

CHAPTER ONE

Elsa doesn't know she's a dog. She is. She certainly looks like one. A one hundred and fifty pound black and white sweetheart who looks like a dog, but thinks, in some strange and striking ways, like a human. Actually like me.

Elsa is a Newfoundland. An ancient breed, Newfoundlands have long been celebrated as children's caretakers and water rescue dogs. Elsa is descended from a noble line of remarkable bitches, remarkable for their beauty, power, structure, movement, temperament, judgment, size, and humanity. She carries their mantle well. Years ago when Elsa was a six month old pup, a trainer was about to teach the command, "lie down." She used the word "plotz" so we knew she was accustomed to working with rough and tough German shepherds. The trainer's method was to pinch the inner ear of the dog and push the puppy to the ground, barking the command, "Plotz." Elsa yelped in pain and dropped down. Then, released on a free command, she jumped up, placed her paws on the trainer's shoulders, and licked her ear. "See," the trainer said, "she didn't mind at all." Horrified, I took Elsa outside and drove away. Of course she minded. What creature doesn't mind pain? Elsa was astonished by a human acting in a cruel manner. Elsa did the right thing. She gave the trainer a lesson in humanity: "Listen, we do not hurt each other. I forgive you."

"We" is the operative word here. We…Elsa and I. Elsa mirrors me, mimics me, studies me, knows my moves and moods, knows more about me than I know about her. She wants to be me. If I had a zipper up my back, she'd climb inside and stay there forever. And in some deep and lonely way, I want to be Elsa, to enter into her universe. She is a better me than I am. As well as she can, she does what I do, anticipates what I will do. She carries a book upstairs to the bedroom because that's what I do, and a shoe downstairs because I put on my shoes to go out. She folds herself into the matching Morris chair when I sit in mine. She climbs into my bed with me, turns over when I turn over. She moves her lips when I speak. Peacemaker and enforcer, she controls the other dogs—the real ones, particularly her enormously powerful father. If they are acting up as in fence-fighting, real fighting, loud barking, mounting one another, she will nail them at the neck, pull at their collars, drag them by their ears, corner them, hustle them back to their kennels, away from the troubles, separate the instigator from the crowd, and break up the fight. When we go to the Cornell Veterinary School she will climb into a chair in the waiting room and be a person. I admire her morality, her steadfastness, her concentration, her righteousness, her exquisite judgment, her enormous efforts to do what I do, to anticipate what I want, what I will do, her devotion, her kindness, and most of all, her strength. But for a dog trying to be a human, to have moderated her own instincts, subsumed them in becoming me, negating her instincts doesn't always work well, particularly if she is about to give birth to seventeen puppies. She needs all the dog instincts in place. They are not.

A thousand years ago when I was four or five, a cat and her kittens took up residence behind the lattice work under my grandmother's porch. I spent a summer trying to talk to them. My parents, my twin sister, and I lived with my mother's parents in a Long Island compound of two sprawling Victorian houses on acres of lawn within walking distance of the Atlantic. We had no pets. The country had just come out of the depression and my grandparents were harboring relatives escaped from Hitler's Germany. The house was too full and frugal for extra dependents. My need to befriend the cats in the dark recesses of the porch was very different than loneliness. It was a yearning that somehow I could pierce their universe, that they would recognize me, agree that "among them all that one's okay," and allow me into their mysterious otherworld behind the green paint of the lattice work under my grandmother's porch. In order to break our language barrier, on my knees, I spent the summer whispering to them: "Milk, fish, eggs, meat. Milk, fish, eggs, meat." They withdrew further into the shadows.

I had already been in serious trouble for pilfering a ball-peen hammer from my grandfather's tool shed and using it to break up the concrete cover of a goldfish pond, covered when my twin sister and I were born. Unimpressed by the logic that the goldfish could no longer be alive, I hammered endlessly on their concrete barrier. I wanted to see them, to set them free. Then, in gratitude, they would tell me their fish secrets, let me into their dimension. When my activity was discovered, I was forced to trade the ball-peen hammer for the more immediate gratification of the whipped cream and sponge cake miracle of a Charlotte Russe in a frilled cardboard cup which, if you push up too hard from the bottom, the whipped cream goes up your nose. I returned to my unrewarding mantra of milk, fish, eggs, and meat.

One of those childhood evenings the burning subject of discussion at the dinner table was of an eccentric lady who lived alone with her dogs in another mansion along the winding road bordering dunes and ocean. She had been found dead by the police. The tone of the adult discussion was that of disapproval, madness, and calamity. The police had counted twenty-seven dogs. Imagine, the conversation went, living alone with twenty-seven dogs. Everyone shook their heads. I was stunned. Living with twenty-seven dogs did not seem to me like living alone. I had no idea what death meant but I knew that living with twenty-seven dogs was my idea of heaven. A thousand years later, still hoping to break through that lattice work separating me from the animals, I have become that eccentric lady, sharing my life with dozens of 150 pound Newfoundlands. I've had my nose pressed against that lattice work all of my life. So has Elsa.

Whatever madness prompts a reasonable human being to become a dog breeder? What prompts a reasonable human being to walk across Antarctica? Why couldn't I just read novels, get pedicures, and play Mahjong on the internet? I think my demon is curiosity. If I put this gorgeous creature together with that gorgeous creature, what kind of puppies will they have? Who will they be? But it's more than that. It's miracle and mystery. I've been a writer all my grown life, but when I became a breeder, I entered into a far deeper mystery—the mystery and miracle of creation: making life. That's a miracle. But death being as great a miracle as birth, I've wrestled with the universe in a landscape that is terrifying, challenging, and ultimately as thrilling: making puppies.

Elsa was obscenely grotesquely pregnant. She was as wide as a beer barrel. She carried a load of puppies, far too many we would find out. Our plan was that Elsa would have a C-section some time just before Thanksgiving. Many breeders opt for C-sections rather than the at-home do-it-yourself horror stories which often require a mad dash, sometimes during winter blizzards, to the vets with puppies stuck in the birth canal. There have been too many horror stories for me to take a chance. Our veterinarian's animal hospital was two hours away. It was far better to be five minutes away. We planned to drive there ahead of time and wait in a nearby motel until Elsa went into heavy stages of labor and then, praying the puppies were ready to survive, get the puppies on the ground.

The night before Thanksgiving, three days earlier than her due date, Elsa went into the first stages of labor. We knew she was carrying a lot of puppies but at that point we didn't know exactly how many. Enormous now, Elsa struggled to climb the two steps of the horse mount at the foot of our bed. As well-decorated as my bedroom is—cherry paneling, stone fireplaces, heavy dark antiques—this uncompromisingly bright blue plastic horse mount designed

4

for little kids trying to climb horses is uncompromisingly ugly. It serves well however to protect dog hips, elbows, and knees. Ordinarily Elsa would forego the horse mount and take one kamikaze leap onto our bed. But now she struggled. She was confused and frightened. Why isn't my body working the way it should? She needed to be with me. Bob and I, trying not to squeeze or push at her enormous breasts or the sagging full belly, pushed, pulled, lifted. She had to weigh 180 pounds by now. At last the big head sunk onto my belly, Elsa sighed mightily and went to sleep. But only for moments. She couldn't get comfortable. She sat up, panted, coughed, drooled, flopped down again only to sit up again. In pain, agitated, definitely in labor. But how advanced? The load of pups had dropped further down toward the birth canal. Elsa's spine seemed elevated above the saddle bags on her sides.

There would be no sleeping for any of us. I started thinking. Now? I went over the due date again. The 23rd of November, give or take two days. This was the night of the 20th. I didn't want to wait; I wanted to be settled in the motel near the vet hospital. In place, nearby, safe. Get up, get dressed, get on the road? Is she just too warm in my bedroom? Is she in pain? Is she in late stage labor or simply going into labor? Wait until morning? Get up and get out now? With all those puppies she could come into labor earlier than calculated. If she broke her water, we had to start delivering. The pups might just arrive as we were on the highway. I wanted to be at the vet's hospital. I worked myself up. I reviewed everything I knew, had experienced, or heard. The Beagle Book, my highly critical title for whatever is taught at veterinary schools about canine reproduction based only on an imprisoned colony of breeding beagles, predicts a drop in temperature, then a rise back to normal, then delivery within twenty-four hours. I don't know how long the drop has to stay dropped. Minutes? Seconds? Do you take the dog's temp every half hour? I've never been able to get this right. And Elsa herself had not read the Beagle Book. I

5

couldn't tell if we missed the drop in temperature or if it had never happened. Was my dog about to break water within hours or within days? Her temperature had fallen and risen and then fallen again. For days. Those few days of living on the edge are harrowing. There is just no telling until the water breaks. But, if you are planning on doing a C-section, and you are two hours away, waiting for that moment is not feasible. And then there should be those tell-tale contractions. Or are there? With Elsa's grandmother I spent a night on the floor of the vet's office, my head on my girl's belly, thinking I would feel the contractions. By the time I woke up, she was already delivering puppies in the surgery room. I know one very experienced breeder who had her dog up on the grooming table, brushing her out. She was not having contractions. Even so, she dropped a puppy standing there on the grooming table. There are rules but no one follows them. You try. You take the temps, watch for contractions, watch for a softening vulva, watch, watch, watch.

Elsa's temperature had fluctuated for days. She was still eating. The Beagle Book insists dogs stop eating when it's time. I had learned that the vulva softens up, expands, and feels like cottage cheese. I would keep checking a container of cottage cheese to compare but never found any measurable consistencies between Crowley's Large Curd Cottage Cheese and Elsa's vulva which actually, happily, was expanding.

Taking the temperature of a long-haired dog is a challenge. First of all, the dog doesn't like it. Secondly, there's no light at the end of that tunnel. We lift the tail and try to find our destination by poking around. I just close my eyes and imagine with my fingers while someone holds the tail up and out of the way. So I continue to take her temperature. Good girl that Elsa is (or perhaps she is merely wary of my aim), when she sees the thermometer in my hand she lifts her tail to let in the light.

The why-nots very quickly out-weighed the whys. Why not? I couldn't sleep anyway. Why not? It was only ten o'clock. Why not? Convinced, I called Mamie whom I had hired a week before, and said, "May as well go. She's getting ready. Let's go."

"Are you sure?"

"Of course not."

Mamie said, "Let's go. Why not? I'll bring Joy."

I knew I would really get to like Mamie's strength. I was very excited, very nervous, very focused, and relieved we would soon be under the protective umbrella of the vet and his staff. Mamie arrived within twenty minutes with Joy in tow.

I served on the board of an animal science program at an alternative technical school; I turned to them to find help with the oncoming incoming. That's how I found Joy, who was a student in her late twenties and, with incredible good fortune, Mamie, who ran the group home Joy lived in. Two weeks earlier, Mamie, who might be described as a cougar, had driven Joy over to my home for the interview. Mamie explained that she ran a group home for mentally disturbed women and Joy was one of the state wards. The others were crazy, Mamie assured me, but Joy, as long as she took her meds, wasn't.

Mamie insisted she could control Joy. I bought the package. Mamie is a handsome, strapping Swedish woman, a garage sale diva, a Maltese breeder, a tough survivor who prefers truck drivers and Karaoke, wears sparkly garage sale findings, and never sleeps at night. "Never sleeps at night" went to the top of her credentials. Joy, who had been studying animal health, behavior, and grooming, had already helped Mamie deliver a Maltese litter. How bad could that be? The director of the Animal Science program told me that Joy went out of her way to help others, loved animals, and was a straight A student. Then, the director's voice dropped, "But she has a history." I didn't care. As a matter of fact I like histories. If I had had a history as dramatic as Joy's, I could have written a bodice-ripping best-seller. I assured myself that

7

because Joy would be living with us, working during the day, sleeping at night, she would be too isolated, too cared for, too busy to get into trouble. And Mamie would be there in case. And we did live in the boonies in a hundred plus acres of forest and field. So we became Elsa's team: Mamie, Joy, and I. Elsa was such a mommy's girl – so humanized -- I didn't know how much help she would be. I didn't think she would be competent as a dog mother.

Mamie would come at night and stay until morning. Joy would cover the days. And I would stay with the pups day and night. For the rush of Elsa's first week we would all work together all the time. We fixed up a guest room, bought a TV set for Joy, found country clothes my daughters had left for their visits, arranged with much paperwork and shifting of protocols with her school that the three months Joy would stay with us caring for the puppies would be Animal Science enough. I agreed, having once been a certified teacher, to fill out report cards and give her tests. If we needed more help, Mamie or the Universe would find more women to help. Hopefully they would not be women Mamie described as her "mentals". I thought perhaps I was casting for Ocean's Eleven.

On that night, when we made the decision to get Elsa to the vet, Joy was lost within her deadening protocol of night time medication. She was silent, monosyllabic, slow-moving, made no eye contact. Knowing very little of her needs, I was still horrified to see what the State does to its wards. I was sure I would know more by the end of our vigils.

We led a recalcitrant Elsa to the car. Movement was so difficult for her. Her body had betrayed her. She leaned against me, then Mamie, then Joy, as if to comfort us, pressing her strength into us, assuring us. We steadied her, pushed and pulled as she dragged herself up the ramp and into the back of the Suburban. It was a great effort. She collapsed on her pile of blankets. Joy lay down next to her. All the what-ifs were in the car already: our suitcases, puppy formula, bottles, blankets, towels, three insulated styrofoam lidded boxes from Omaha Steak because in preparation for the onslaught of visitors, workers, and hungry husbands we would need plenty of prepared frozen foods. The boxes would be perfect for bringing home puppies. We were also carrying snacks for us, drinks for us, warm jackets and boots, scissors and dental floss to tie off umbilical cords, hot water bottles, and infant formula just in case Elsa delivered while we were on the road. Mamie offered to drive. I let her. I hadn't a full night's sleep in days. It was snowing lightly. Mamie seemed thoroughly competent and confident.

There are not many moments in life when one is called upon to be present in the deepest sense. On that bitter cold November night, driving into a snow storm, I was present, fully present, powerful, prepared, ready to fight with any weapon I had for the lives of Elsa's puppies. Perhaps heroic. Going to the valley of death to bring forth life. I was ready to do battle with the very stars, to pull those puppies from nothingness to life, to enter some mysterious beyond of life and death, of destiny, to wrestle with the angels for the lives of Elsa's puppies. Why would I choose this terrifying challenge when I could be getting pedicures and playing Mahjong? What errant gene, what lust do Elsa and I each have that we need to go to the edge of our comfortable world and enter another's universe?

Elsa's snores had turned to rumbles. Since restlessness is one of the signs of serious labor and Elsa was no longer restless, I could go to sleep. I lay my head back on the neck rest of the car, said a short prayer that the snow wouldn't get heavier, that Elsa wouldn't have puppies in the car, that I would have the strength and endurance to care for Elsa and her puppies. I drifted into a welcome sleep.

Mamie drove north through the ever increasing snowfall. I woke up now and then to hear her talking melodically and happily about life and men, mostly men, mostly truck drivers, mostly garage sales, mostly her thirty-one knee operations, mostly her career in the mental hospital and how exciting it was. I figured anyone who can control a six foot paranoid schizophrenic guy without getting her jaw broken can certainly deal with a few inches of snow.

Until I felt the car brake, felt it slide. "We're okay. We're okay," Mamie told herself.

Red lights flashed in front of us. A tractor trailer was jack-knifed in the left lane, its cab in the median. "Stay to the right; fourth gear," I advised Mamie but she had already shifted down. "Don't stop. Keep going."

"Shouldn't we stop to see if he's okay?"

"We can't. We just can't. And there might be other cars sliding into us. Keep going." The sense of sudden death, the uncertainty of destiny, of event, the fear I already carried with me with all those unborn puppies almost present and their compromised mother increased as we crept forward. Suddenly, I was scared. My intellectual what-ifs melted into emotional what's-nexts. My grid of confidence, trust, and control disintegrated. I had been so well-prepared, so beautifully organized, so in charge. One tries so hard to control life and then swiftly events spin out of control. The puppies were on the shaky cusp of life, so close to death, so close to never making it to life. Anything could go wrong. Ten minutes delay on the road could mean death for the puppies. I could not be distracted. I had to maintain, jaws clenched, a narrow focus, an absolutely narrow focus, no drift, no imagining. Death rode on my shoulder. I was at war with death. I was delivering life. I had to be brave. I had to be Elsa.

CHAPTER TWO

At last we pulled into the icy parking lot of Rocky Graziano's World Famous Motel across the road from The Boxing Hall of Fame. We helped all 180 pounds of Elsa out of the car, down the ramp. She was so awkward and huge and uncomfortable. As difficult as this was for her, she offered us her usual patience and trust by leaning into each of us and pressing against our knees. I thought at the moment I had abused her trust, putting her through this pregnancy. I led her gently to a snow covered area to pee. She wandered but did not pee. She stood still for me as I examined her rear end for green or black which would mean the pups had died, for blood which I don't know what it would mean but would be bad, and for remnants of the mucous plug which would indicate her water was about to break. Nothing. That was the good news. The bad news was that she had not produced any urine. There were no little yellow holes in the snow. That worried me. A lot. Not unlike an icicle through my heart. Her water bucket in the car was empty. Why didn't she pee? Maybe, just maybe, because it was a strange place and she was uneasy. Or something systemic wasn't working. We'd unpack, settle in, and take her out again. This was the beginning of a long and terrible night.

There was no telling why Rocky Graziano's World Famous Hotel is world famous unless, on the occasion of the annual Boxing Hall of Fame awards ceremony, world famous boxers with multiple damaging concussions holed up there across the highway from the Hall of Fame building. They might not have noticed the rubbery pillows, the thin stiff blankets and the see-through bath towels, or even felt the

11

deep vertical rift in the center of the mattresses. I've slept in far worse and far better places and am only amused at what circumstance dishes out to me. I can sleep anywhere. But not that night.

Elsa immediately claimed the narrow space between the two beds. Joy claimed the bed next to the heater and went back to sleep. I'm not sure she'd ever been totally awake. She packed some heavy meds. Mamie laid out a party of cut veggies, dips, chips, and crackers on a small round table and turned on the TV. We had enough onion dip and underwear to last for the four days we might possibly stay. I led Elsa outside again. She hadn't peed in hours. I pulled a towel from the bathroom to take with me just in case Elsa pushed a puppy out when she squatted. Elsa went dutifully, painfully, squatted, produced nothing, let me lead her back to the building. It had taken Elsa only one time to learn to wait until the clerk opened the door from a button on her desk, only once to know which door in the long hallway belonged to our room. She was such a good girl, pushy, but good-natured. She was doing this for me and I felt increasingly guilty for what I was putting her through.

We gave her fresh water and she drank it up, panted, lay down in her spot, rolled from side to side to get comfortable. She slept as briefly as I did. Mamie pulled a chair over to the bathroom, turned on the single bulb bathroom light and read a book I'd written. Neither of us had taken our clothes off. Elsa snored deeply, woke up to pant, sat up, lay down, sat up, panted, groaned, grunted, slept a few minutes, sat up, panted. I slept fitfully as did poor Elsa, praying morning would come soon. We turned on the air conditioning. The room was freezing. But Elsa continued to pant. Was this just restlessness, pain, or final stages of labor? This seemed more than restlessness. I allowed myself to sleep for a few minutes. Mamie shook me awake. "Elsa did something. Something happened. She made a big uuhh sound. Something hurt her. This isn't right."

I turned all the lights on and lifted Elsa's chin. She wouldn't look in my eyes. This was so unlike her. She lives for eye contact. "What are you trying to tell me, Elsa? What do you want me to do? I am so sorry. I am so sorry." She looked at me and licked my hand. I knew by now, while she might be in the final stages of labor, there was something else very serious going on. Call the vet? It's two in the morning. Call? Maybe she'll go to sleep. Wait until morning? Was it Elsa who couldn't wait until morning or was it me? "Mamie, wake up Joy. Let's get ready. I'm going to call. Let's pack in case we have to go in now."

While we waited for mildly dysfunctional Joy to shake off her meds, wake up, and get dressed, we continued to doubt our actions. Perhaps our doubts, our ignorance, had precipitated our actions? Mamie's little Maltese dogs hide under the bed, have their puppies without assistance, and take care of them. Mamie had never gone through this. I had but I've never been sure and most times I've made stupid premature neurotic decisions. Perhaps the panting meant she was just pushing, a period in later stages of labor but not the latest, getting ready but not ready yet. Elsa didn't make the 'uhhh' sound again. We waited. Mamie and I put on our ski jackets and went outside with her, held onto each other as we crossed the icy parking lot to a snow bank. The glow of lights from McDonald's lit our way, turned the ice field bloody with the liquid reds of birth, death and Big Macs. I needed to turn my imagination off. I needed to turn my fear off. There is a syndrome psychologists have identified: once you believe in something, everything you see from then on conforms to that belief; even when it's wrong, it's factual. The gremlin in you registers nothing else but what you want to or must believe. Everything is a sign, a terrifying sign.

I swiped Elsa's bottom. She had done nothing, not a drop. How could she have drunk the buckets and buckets of water and have no urine? I knew she had to be seen. There was something other than labor going on. Should I call the

13

doctor? Should I wait? What if I'm wrong and I've woken him up? What if this is normal and I'm just being utterly stupid? I reviewed everything I could remember about pregnancies. No. I had to call. The urination and drinking were symptomatic of something not so good. I called.

"Is this an emergency?" a woman asked groggily.

"No," I really wanted to say. "I'm just lonely." I controlled myself. Stupidity as well as boredom brings out the worst in me. I described Elsa's symptoms, my concerns. I hoped the woman would stay awake long enough to call the vet. I prayed that one of the really experienced vets was on call that night.

There are twelve vets in Dr. Brown's office. A week earlier when I brought Elsa abnormally, abysmally swollen, in for a final check-up, the newest, youngest vet had asked politely, "Now, why is Elsa here today?" Perhaps she was just following the official office greeting protocol. However, not recognizing a pregnancy that was so grossly obvious put me on alert and alarm. It did not bode well for this moment. I hoped she wouldn't be the one who would be calling back.

Joy was again or still asleep. Mamie, because of her years working in the mental institution, was tough. She threatened, shouted, pulled off Joy's blankets, and shook her. Threatened with getting her hair pulled out, Joy actually sat up and put on her ski jacket. We had swept all the snacks back into the cooler; our suitcases were in the car. At last the phone rang. It was indeed the youngest and newest vet. I described the symptoms. She paused. I could hear her breathing as she thought through my information and made her decision carefully and professionally. "Bring her in. I'll be there in fifteen minutes." There was something firm in her voice, something slightly reassuring.

We loaded Elsa back into the car, pushing her up the ramp. Mamie slipped and fell on the ice. I was alarmed but she stood up strong and brave. I was so grateful for her strength. She was certainly what one would call a trouper, whatever 'trouper' means. Elsa sighed as she sank down in the rear of the car, relieved to be in a familiar place. Poor poor baby. I started talking to the Universe, making deals, negotiating destinies, praying. In the rear of the Suburban, Joy, towel in hand, turned her flashlight onto Elsa, to watch, just in case.

    The parking lot of the vet hospital was dark. I was incredibly relieved to see Kerry and Nicky Brown's cars at the far end of the parking lot, which meant they were home. Dr. Brown's house is attached to the back of the hospital. All their house lights were off. A single light shone inside the hospital office. A car pulled up. In my headlights I recognized a vet tech I'd known for years. She rushed into the building. The lights went on in the building. Another tech arrived. And two more. The young doctor arrived within fifteen minutes and told us to bring Elsa in. She wasted no time. She took Elsa's temp. It was 106. It should be 101 to 102. Quickly recognizing an emergency, she woke Dr. Brown up. She said infection. I didn't think so. She set up two intravenous bags, one on each of Elsa's legs. Kerry was with us in minutes, Kerry rubbed his eyes, woke himself up, took a look, asked me exactly when she was due, the exact days of breeding, told me to call home and double-check, determined in a flash that the puppies were probably ready. Until their lungs are ready to work, they can't survive. A day too early, the lungs are stuck together and the puppy is simply unable to breathe. A day too late, the pups are already dead. There's a very tight window. That's why the timing of the breeding date is so important. These puppies were a day early. But ready or not, we had no options other than to take them. Dr. Brown decided Elsa was just dehydrated, running a fever because her systems had shut down, not infected, which was a relief. There were already enough problems to deal with.

I called Bob, woke him up, asked him to look at the records to make certain what the exact days of breeding were. I waited, my heart pounding, my face hot with terror. The dates were not good news. It was clear: Elsa wasn't ready to deliver yet. And if Elsa wasn't ready to deliver, there was a good chance the puppies wouldn't survive. We were only a few days early but those days were the difference between life and death. I remember clutching the phone in the darkened office, my hands trembling, my elbows on the cold counter, my chin quivering.

"Save Elsa," Bob said. "She can make more puppies. Save Elsa."

If asked to make that decision, I too would have opted to save Elsa and let the puppies go. As I write this, I realize how easy it is to say now. I don't know how well I could have lived with that decision. I remember the moment in the motel room when Elsa made her UHHH sound, as if someone had hit her in the belly. UHHH was the way I felt.

By the time I returned with the breeding dates in hand, Elsa's temperature was stabilizing. Elsa was wheeled past me into the operating room. "It's going to be okay, sweetheart. It's going to be wonderful," I lied. "You're going to have puppies. Puppies!" As the techs led her away, she looked over her shoulder at me and my heart broke. I had to turn my back so she wouldn't see that I was weeping. I tried to assure myself that we needed puppies to support the kennel, that Elsa was such a magnificent contribution to the gene pool she had to be replicated, and so on. I wasn't assured. I felt -- well, I felt guilty. Terribly guilty. Why was I doing this to her? To satisfy my own creative hunger? My pleasure? It was not the time to ask the questions.

I was trying not to cry, shaking. I knew it was a life and death moment. Nicky Brown, the doctor's wife -- herself a vet tech -- arrived, asked me to come into the room just beyond the surgery room. I didn't think I could. I've seen this view before -- other dogs that weren't my own open and

16

bloody on the surgery table, tongue hanging over the edge of the table. If I were to see my Elsa like so much meat, I might pass out and become yet another problem. I could help with the puppies which I'd done before, but one glimpse of Elsa looking dead and bloody would be unbearable. Somehow I had to steel myself not to look into the surgery room. I imagined Kerry holding the uterus up in the air and pulling out puppies like peas from a bloody pod. My knees weakened. Ice water flowed through my legs. I had to turn my imagination off, stay in the moment, be present. I've fainted before at the sight of blood. Mamie, however, was up for it, excited. "Come on. Come on." She was thrilled to participate, a little too thrilled, I thought. But then she was accustomed to handling mental patients who no one else could control and confessed she loved the excitement. Well, there was plenty for her. Too much for me.

"I can't, Mamie. I might faint." I was also concerned that Mamie, in her freight-train power, might try to take over and offend Nicky.

"But they need you now," Mamie insisted. "The puppies."

Their need was a different story. I took my place in the room just beyond the surgery room. Six of us stood waiting at a long, stainless steel examination table: Nicky, Joy, Mamie, I, and two vet techs. Nicky gave orders like a field commander. The incubators were on and warming. The acupuncture needles, little bottles of Dr. Bach's Rescue Remedy, oxygen, towels were laid out at one end of the table. Rescue Remedy is a human homeopathic medicine. Hard to believe it works or even why it works, but it works to stabilize the system. I've taken it myself, given it to dogs who have had some kind of trauma or are nervous just prior to going into the show ring. The explanation is that it contains the vibrations of certain flowers (their energy) which re-establishes the vibrational balances of other living systems. Is this why we send flowers to sick people? Is this why a

Neanderthal burial, hundreds of thousands of years old, contained certain kinds of flowers? I'll bet it was for a Neanderthalian reason far beyond sentiment. What I love about veterinarians as opposed to the doctors who treat humans is that so many of them are willing to try many things and, if something works, they use it. It doesn't matter why or how it works or what else it was designed to do, just that it works. If the vibrations of flowers and three drops of brandy steady your nerves and reduce heart rate, why not?

I thought perhaps I wouldn't be very useful, that I might make a mistake, drop a baby. You see, I didn't think Elsa would survive. And I had done this to her. I could barely see past my tears. I took a swig of Rescue Remedy.

The surgery was going on just beyond us. From the quick glance I dared take, I could see two vets and two technicians bent over the surgery table. Thank God I couldn't see Elsa past them. Another technician stood in the doorway between our rooms. I knew the process. Kerry would cut my Elsa open, remove the uterus, and pull out puppies. Elsa, my poor baby. Then the surgery room tech would rush the puppy to the tech at the doorway who would remove whatever was left of the caul, wipe the puppy off, afterbirth, slime, blood, mucous. It was all too graphic. Somehow I managed not to watch. I couldn't stop imagining. I swigged six drops of the puppies' Rescue Remedy. The puppies would get only one drop. The normal human dose is three drops. I wasn't a normal human that night.

"Here they come," Kerry yelled to us. The tech manning the door passed us the first puppy. Kerry called again from the surgery room, words muffled under his surgical mask. "Rhoda, do you know how many puppies there are in here?"

"At least ten. The sonogram team at Cornell said at least ten."

"A lot more than ten, Rhoda. A lot more."

18

The first puppy was breathing, a tiny acupuncture needle stuck under its pink nostrils. And complaining noisily, mad as hell, as my mother would say. Hooray for life. It was a beautiful puppy.

"With a nasty temper," someone joked and I had to laugh through the tears.

"Girl," Nicky announced.

Someone else corrected her, joked. "Bitch."

I was not up to joking. Nicky passed the pup to me, most likely to comfort me. I held it to my nose and blew into her face to introduce myself or offer her air. I don't to this day know which. She nuzzled to suck my nose. "Welcome, baby. Welcome. It's going to be okay." I was assuring myself. "Thank you. Thank you, God, for this life." Another puppy arrived, was passed to me.

The vet tech, her voice flat, said, "Needs work," and turned back for the next one from the surgery room. The one I had wasn't moving.

"Come on, Puppy, take a breath. Come on. Come on. You can do this. Come on. Live! Dear God, please grant this little thing life. Please." The puppy remained rag-doll limp. Nicky pulled it from my hands, put it on oxygen. Its chest moved.

Suddenly we all had puppies in our hands, rubbing them shaking them, praying, laughing as they yelled in their new fury. "I'm here! I'm here. I am! And I am no longer comfortable!" And more puppies. And more puppies. Soon three, soon four, soon five, were ready for the incubators. A tech stood at the incubator with her hand in the opening, rubbing rubbing, rubbing, to stimulate them. Some, either not quite ready to use their lungs or still dopey from Elsa's anesthesia, needed more work to wake up. I glanced at Mamie who had been so good about waking up Joy. She was as good at waking up the puppies although didn't threaten them. She swung and rubbed them with great confidence. She was rubbing mightily, smiling, hovering over

19

everything, learning, monitoring Joy, giving her support and affirmation, taking orders from Nicky without hesitation. We passed those we couldn't wake up to Nicky, and magically, marvelously, she brought them to life with oxygen, acupuncture, and far more vigorous swinging to and upward from the floor than any of us other than Mamie dared. Each received a drop of Rescue Remedy before they entered the incubator. Kerry called out to us. "One horn's done. I'm starting on the next."

Footnote: although this brutal shaking and swinging to release whatever liquids remain in the lung, and has accomplished this in the past, this time-honored procedure has obviously become suspect and is no longer done. Now we just rub the daylights out of them. I suspect there is less brain damage. I was always suspicious of it.

"How many so far?" I asked Nicky. She counted the crowd in the incubator. "Nine. In one horn."

"Oh, God," I said under my breath. "What have I done?"

The uterus has two horns. I have always thought the ancient horned cow-goddesses of the Middle-East represented the miraculous connection to the power of life, to the miracle, represented the uterus. The statues of the cow goddess Hathor's head is shaped remarkably like a uterus…and in her ears --seeds. Moses himself was supposed to have horns and there was some peculiar issue about a golden calf out there in the Sinai desert. Do horns represent fallopian tubes? Okay, how many puppies can fit in a fallopian tube? Does Elsa have too many? What's too many? My rule of thumb is one puppy for each nipple. Eight to ten is about it. We were out of the comfort zone.

"Is Elsa okay?" I called in, couldn't help myself. I'm sure civilians like me are not entirely welcome in the mysterious back rooms of the vet hospital.

"Doing fine," one of the techs answered, probably placating me.

I heard Kerry call out, "This horn's filled too!"

Twenty puppies? Eighteen? We would be bottle-feeding around the clock.

And more puppies. Ours was a combination five- star fire alarm bucket brigade and a mass production line. Nicky kept announcing "Girl. Boy." I lost track. They were all beautiful. The puppies were howling and clucking. "I'm here. I'm here. I am!" And more puppies. It was amazing that no one dropped a puppy, slithery, mucous-covered as they were, as we passed them on, or kept them to swing up and down from waist to floor. Two more people arrived, took their places at the incubator, stuck their hands into the opening, rubbed the puppies. One of the incubator crew I recognized as Kerry and Nicky's daughter. She had just returned from college minutes before and come down to help. I could see puppies moving, creeping, lifting their heads, searching. Actually moving, moving, alive, real. "Where the hell are we?" Are puppies able to smell when they are in the womb? Is this their first smell experience? Consciousness? I had ruined everyone's Thanksgiving, but I gave thanks again and again: they were born and breathing, settled and safe in the incubator.

Years before I had been invited to witness a gorilla birth at the Calgary Zoo. The mother, Julia, had been hand-raised by a friend/curator at the Toronto Zoo. With a revolving team of curators and vets, we waited for days watching Julia on a video screen. At last, at long last, Julia stood up to deliver her baby. We cheered. Someone, certainly one of the men, yelled, "Touchdown!" Julia lay back and beat

21

her chest with her fists, drumming her joy to the universe. I felt Julia's joy then and I felt it there with Elsa's new puppies. I felt it rising hysterically in my chest and thought I too had to beat it down and contain it because I wanted to leave and call Bob and tell him so far so good.

And then, finally, Kerry called out to us, to me, "Elsa's okay. Her signs are good. She's fine. This has to be a record. How many did we get?"

I wanted to say so much to him. I wanted to lick his hand, but I didn't know how to begin. Good Lord, I was thinking like a dog.

Nicky went to count the crowded incubator. "Seventeen."

"All okay?"

"All okay," she answered matter-of-factly as if their survival were a given. The puppies had piled up on each other. They were cold. Nicky adjusted the heat in the incubator. They separated, as primitive as a slime mold.

Through the large window of the surgery room overlooking the parking lot, I could see that dawn now filled the sky. It was Thanksgiving morning. It had been a long, long night. Kerry came out, leaned against the edge of a counter, slowly pulled off his surgical gloves as if his hands were hurting, pulled his surgical mask down. His face was pale. His hair damp with perspiration. He was very tired.

"You're a very lucky woman, Rhoda. If you'd waited until morning, we would have lost them all. All, Rhoda. All of the puppies and Elsa. Very lucky. She tore her uterus. She was about to burst. We would have lost them all."

I looked at Mamie. She nodded. That was the 'uhhh' sound Elsa had made which had alarmed Mamie and precipitated our call to the vet. Elsa's uterus had ripped open.

I buried my face in my hands, wiped my eyes with my sleeves, and went to the incubator. Rather respectfully, I thought, the techs stepped aside. I reached into the opening and touched each puppy. I had to touch them all, welcoming them, connecting with them, because I was searching for the return of souls I had loved. I knew my dogs who had left (as the psychics say) were out there in the ether, up there, waiting to occupy one of these new-born bodies with their angelic souls. I just couldn't yet tell which was going to be which, who was going to be who. They sucked my fingers. "They're hungry," I announced. It was over, but it had just begun.

I called Bob, woke him up.

"What time is it?"

"Seventeen," I said.

"Seventeen." Then he really woke up. "Seventeen?" he said again and hung up, called back. "Seventeen?"

"Yes, seventeen."

"How many boys?"

"We're not sure."

"Seventeen. God help us."

CHAPTER THREE

The incubation room was a frenzy of activity. People were feeding puppies, stimulating them, cleaning them, shaking them, weighing them, recording descriptions, calling friends and family on their cell phones, taking pictures. "Seventeen," I heard people on their phones. "Yes, seventeen. And they're all okay." We were news. The sun arrived. The wind blew the snow into corners. They sky was blue, without a cloud. The day shift arrived. Thanksgiving arrived. My friend Joyce arrived. Joyce is retired from Middle Management at IBM and is steady as a rock. I can always use some extra management "Seventeen. And they're all okay," echoed through the hospital. "Take a picture. Get it on the computer." In a hospital, any hospital, human or animal, there is so much sickness and death, births, remarkable births such as Elsa's, make everyone happy. Elsa, Mamie reported, stitched together again, lay on a gurney, covered with blankets, shaking and shivering as the anesthesia left her system. Still I didn't look. Mamie insisted that she had watched a lot of the delivery in the surgery room and never saw any blood. I didn't believe her. Without looking, I felt I had seen too much already. I was protecting myself. Happiness and fear are uneasy companions.

Kerry came into the incubator room. "Go wait someplace. You have two very little girls. They'll need to be fed every hour. Don't give up on them. We'll bring them to you." I walked around three or four corners until I came to a small room with a built in bench and a picture window next to the parking lot. I folded myself into the bench, knees up to my chin, pressed my hands over my face, and steadied myself.

A young, grinning vet tech came into the room with silver chocolate kisses, told me where I could find more, returned, reported that everything was going well, I popped as many chocolate kisses as fast as I could. If Rescue Remedy stabilizes, just think what Hershey's Kisses can do. And then I looked out the windows to the parking lot, to what had been a cloudless blue sky, but what was suddenly not a cloudless blue sky, and leaped up and ran to the incubator room... "Joyce! Joyce, get your camera."

The puppies, fed, stabilized, creeping around, were still in the incubator. I grabbed Joyce's arm and dragged her through rooms to get to the window of the whelping room. "What's the matter?" What could be more important than the puppies?

I pointed to the sudden single cloud above the parking lot. "Pippa. Pippa made a cloud. Pippa came to help." It was the great head of a large white Newfoundland, completely familiar.

"What?" Joyce, after all a practical woman, shook her head.

"The cloud, Joyce! Look at the cloud!" Its shape was already beginning to soften. But it was still very clear what we were looking at. "It's Pippa. It must be Pippa. She promised the animal psychic she'd be back to help Elsa and here she is."

"Oh my God," Joyce whispered the awe I felt. "Oh my God, it's a Newf. It's a Newf head. It's exactly a Newf head. How could that be? Camera. Camera." Joyce filmed Pippa's cloud until it floated over the picket fence. The sky was once again utterly cloudless. We stood at the window, waiting for more clouds. There were none. Joyce nudged me. "Who's Pippa?"

"One of my old ladies, dead ten years. I named her for a little girl in a Victorian play who sings a song as she passes. 'Morning's at seven. God's in his Heaven. All's right with the world.' It couldn't have been a better message. "All's right with the world. She said she'd come back. To help."

25

"Said to who?" Joyce rolled her eyes. She'd already abandoned her church. She didn't need any more of this. I couldn't expect people to dance in the ether with me. Management, IBM, that she was, she said, "Seventeen puppies. How are you going to do this?"

We hugged. "God's in his heaven. All's right with the world." Pippa kept her promise to help. I needed no proof. Pippa had come back. Anything was possible. I was walking on air. The Universe was delivering.

Then I went in to see Elsa. Everything was fine. Everything would be fine: we'd had a sign from the universe, a promising sign.

Thank God Joyce had her camera and caught the cloud. No one would have believed me: too much chocolate, too little sleep, too much imagination. Oh, and the mercury madness from all the tuna fish sandwiches I'd been chain-eating.

Kerry, pulling off his surgery hat, came in. "All good. Seventeen and Elsa's fine. We're cleaning up the pups. We'll bring them in as soon as they're stable."

When Elsa was led back in the whelping room, groggy, wobbly, she made brief eye contact, no more than a flicker of recognition, and went to sleep. Had she said with her eyes, how can you do this to me? Or, Hi, Mom, I'm okay? Or both? We covered her with blankets as she shivered off the effects of the anesthesia, slowly reclaiming her body and her consciousness. Then the technicians brought the boxes of puppies in. I wept with joy and relief, placed a squealing pup at her nose. "Look, Elsa, puppies!" Without interest she sniffed the odd smell and went back to sleep. We waved a dollop of the liver black bloody afterbirth in front of her nose. The afterbirth is supposed to turn on the bitch's hormones. Forget it. Elsa dropped her head down to the floor. No instinct; no interest. The puppies were far more eager. As soon as we placed their tiny heads onto nipples, they were suckling, kneading the flesh around the nipple, little oil pumps in a perfect black and white row. Elsa slept, snored. I turned to look at the sky over the parking lot. Had I truly seen Pippa's cloud?

"You saw it, Joyce?"

"Yes. I still have goose bumps just talking about it. It's the weirdest thing. Bizarre. I can't stop thinking about it. I want to believe. I have to believe because I saw it."

Everyone always wants to believe but until you see it and get the message, you're never really sure what's true and what isn't true. Once you've seen the cloud, nothing can ever be the same again. Elsa wasn't alone because Pippa, as she had promised, was there.

The pups were pushing their way out of the blankets, eager to smell whatever was out there, eager for life.

Footnote: On the questionable subject of synchronicity versus coincidence, consider these two events. One of our young male dogs died suddenly and unexpectedly. His owner called within the hour. Within the same hour the husband of a woman who cared for him as a puppy arrived to complete some carpentry work. He carried a large flat stone his wife had found in the woods months before. It was a perfect oh-my-God bas relief of a handsome Newfoundland head. And one day, long after Pippa died, I was antiquing with a friend who happened to owe me 130 dollars. We wandered into a consignment shop with many nooks and crannies. She went one way, I the other. And there, hanging in a dusty corner, a large, old chalk drawing of Pippa's look alike, whoever she was. The price was of course 130 dollars. I bought it immediately and called Mary Long, our friendly animal communicator, to talk to Pippa. Pippa said, "Do you know how hard it was to get that to you?" Pippa's cloud didn't astonish me. It satisfied me. The universe works in many ways. Of course, coincidence exists. But if you're paying attention synchronicity also exists.

Because Elsa had so precipitously delivered her pups, changing all of our plans, we'd had no sleep. We were too tired to drive ourselves home, gallons of coffee or not. Not only did we need someone to drive us, we needed a second person to deliver the driver to us. Even though our animals' needs must be met every day, nobody was working that day. So Bob couldn't come in to drive us home. He had to exercise and feed the dozen dogs at home and get the room ready for the puppies. There aren't too many people one can call at 4 in the morning to drive the four hours on winter highways on Thanksgiving. Dave and his family would become major players in the National Newfoundland Disaster.

Dave Hamlin and Greg, his son-in-law-to-be, arrived, bearing a treasure of Dunkin Donuts and coffee. I met the Hamlins soon after we moved to Port Crane. Vicky Hamlin taught fourth grade. She called out of the blue to ask if she could bring the fourth grade to the Dog Farm for a field day. Since my dream had always been that the Budweiser horses would visit me, this was close. Three big yellow school buses pulled into the driveway and children poured out. Vicky's husband, Dave, came and watched. The dogs were thrilled to see children. The children were thrilled to see the dogs. It wasn't long before the Hamlins bought their first Newfy and we'd been close ever since. I knew Dave would help me and Vicky would understand. There was much to be thankful for that Thanksgiving morning particularly the Boston Creme donut which I washed down with shaking hands and more of the puppies' Rescue Remedy. No sooner had Dave and his son-in-law stomped snow off their boots, and washed their hands, they had a tiny puppy and a tiny bottle of formula thrust at them. I showed them how to pry the mouth open and press the nipple between the strong and stubborn jaws. The puppy had to be convinced that milk really could arrive in this strange way. The puppies caught on very quickly. Greg caught on faster than Dave who was being too gentle. Greg had had an adventurous career as a bouncer in a ghetto bar which didn't prepare him for interacting with newborns that fit easily into the palm of his hand. Nevertheless, he was in love and as careful as a lace-maker. Dave told us later he was amazed that anything could be so small, its potential so perfectly organized, that the creature he pressed against his chest as he fed would be as huge as his own Duncan. "Small and perfect," we agreed. I checked the belly on his puppy. It was round and full. Back to the incubator. Nicky thrust a limp puppy at Dave. "Shake him. Make him squeal." Gingerly, cautiously, Dave swung the puppy to the floor. Nicky called out from her incubator station. "You're not doing it right. Make him SQUEAL! Harder." The pup squealed furiously. It was delicious to see those big men handling those tiny pups so carefully and lovingly. I'm from the generation in which, once in a great while, the husband holds the baby but only when asked. Things have obviously changed.

After lesson number one – how to get the puppies to breathe—lesson number two was getting them to suck on a nipple. Lesson number three was feeling the stomach to see if it was full. Lesson four was burping. Lesson five was all over Dave's shirt. We cleaned him and each other up. I remember he wore a beautiful light blue denim shirt with a Newfoundland embroidered over the pocket. I thought it was sweet that he'd wear the "family" clothes. The little room was filled with laughter and jokes. Now, everything was funny. We took turns at naming the puppies. Obviously they became Pumpkin, Turkey, Pilgrim. "Prymouth Rock," I offered. Everyone stopped to look at me. "Prymouth as in Pry the mouth open Rock, as in pry the mouth open to get the nipple in. "Oh," they responded politely and went back to their work. I was perfectly stupid with joy and exhaustion.

I asked Dave much later what I was like that morning. Was I hysterical? Pushy? Short-tempered? No. He said I was very focused. As a novelist, I drift into imaginary worlds more often that not. There was no drifting then or for weeks thereafter. Mamie remembered me as passive, moving deliberately from one thing to the next. I, who am so often distracted in my novelist's head, distracted enough to store the milk in the microwave for example, had somehow risen to the occasion and, for the duration of the Newfoundland National Disaster, had indeed left my imagination behind. Of course, who could have imagined this?

Before the puppies were due, I had crocheted a single line of necklaces for the puppies in all colors of wool: no crochet hook, just slipping one loop into the other and knotting the end. This way we could tell the puppies apart. I would have to make a new set every week as they grew or as the necklaces were lost in the blankets. I calmed myself, praying in my odd way, as if I were handling prayer beads. I had made a dozen and then, just in case, added some. I wept as I made them, wept with joy. As I worked the wool between my fingers, I talked to the puppies about being born and what fun they'll have, and prayed that they would all be big, healthy, gorgeous, loyal dogs with long lives and do good work. When I was pregnant with my oldest daughter, a cat climbed onto my well-developed stomach and kneaded it. My daughter answered, pushing back to the cat. I knew there was consciousness in Elsa's womb, something reaching out, curious, impatient for the next what's next.

At last, the puppies born, breathing, moving about in the incubators, I was able to spread the necklaces on the examining table and we "dressed" each puppy. I didn't have enough different colors (there would never be enough colors) so we doubled up strands of red and white, green and red (who immediately became Ms. Christmas) and so on. Then we noted their markings, sex, and weight. The weights varied between a pound and a pound and a half which is normal and, with seventeen puppies, miraculous. Poor Elsa, poor Elsa's uterus. We had to count again and again. The little pink sex organs look so much alike in the beginning, we continued to make errors and recount. "Did you count this one? I'm not sure. Nicky, come over here and tell us what this is." Just when we thought we had an accurate count, someone would grab a pup to feed or put back in the incubator or the necklace had slid off the tiny head. And we started over again. Finally we organized them. Eleven boys, six girls. Someone suggested ten boys, seven girls. I said we'd find out eventually. We were short three necklaces. So the markings of the un-necklaced pups were recorded: black with four white feet, white with two black spots on its back, black with a white fur necklace. I always seem to put pink, red and dark blue necklaces on the puppies I like best. And, at that moment, I could tell. Other breeders report this as well: the minute the pups are born, the breeders know which one they want or at least which one they will watch carefully. In natural births, as opposed to C-sections, the soft bones of the heads are squeezed by the narrow passage and it is therefore difficult to see the real shape of the head until a few days. But in the C-section, of course, one can tell immediately. What we are looking for are large heads, like little bowling balls, and big bones. Personally I also look for eyes that are far apart, indicating a spread of bone. Greg was already choosing his own puppy, Ms. Red. I had chosen Mr. Dark Blue.

"Why Dark Blue?" Greg asked.

"Because he's marked just as his father so he may be as powerfully built as his father, because maybe he'll have the same saint-like personality as his father, because his head is going to be massive, and his neck is elegantly long. So, why Ms. Red for you, Greg?"

He offered the best reason possible. "Because she's adorable."

She was. They all were. Joy welled up into my chest. I've had that sensation or that message from the Universe twice before: once in Ireland at the edge of a small bay when I watched dolphins come in from the Irish Sea before a storm. And again walking toward the park near my house on July 4th to see fireworks. A rising of ecstasy, rising into my chest, remarkable, perhaps, dare I even suggest, cosmic. I have often wondered how I could bring it on myself. There has never been a way. I hesitate to define it, but I think it is something that comes to me externally. Not relief, not happiness, not pride, but a physical joy, something Eastern religions seem to know more about achieving in ways that might include living as a hermit in a cave and/or standing on your head for six months. I guess I was too earth-bound and would have to go on having puppies. Maybe what I felt was what the gorilla mother Julia felt that day in the Calgary Zoo when she first saw her new baby and drummed on her chest with her fists.

Elsa had very little milk. There was no reason to stay at the vet's any longer. We topped the puppies off with warm formula, packed hot water bottles and towels, tucked the puppies into the insulated boxes, called Bob to turn up the heat in the basement. Plastic jars filled with hot water lay at the bottom of the boxes, then a layer of towels, then a layer of puppies, a blanket, and then the box covers, slightly open. All the puppies had been fed and could go another two hours. It was a two hour drive home. Even so we had formula in baby bottles tucked into the boxes to keep warm. The car could break down. There could be a tie-up on the highway. What if, what if.

We heated the car up into the 90's, led groggy Elsa up her ramp into the car. Joy climbed in with her. Elsa settled into the car, barely aware of us or herself, which was just as well. The men rushed the boxes of puppies out into the cold, pushed them into the area behind the driver's seat, and Mamie climbed in with them. I sat in the front with the donuts. We shed our coats and then our fleece pullovers and plunged into the heavy Thanksgiving traffic on our victory ride home.

The roads were clear. I was still on a high from seeing Pippa's cloud. I didn't want to think about what was ahead of us. Laughter, chocolate, and tuna fish welled up in my chest. "You hear about the woman who asked for a windfall and a tree landed on her head? You have to be very specific when you ask the Universe for something."

"How many did you ask for?"

"I just said plenty. Plenty of puppies. I should have asked for eight." I quickly added. "But don't get me wrong, Universe. I'm very happy with all of them. Thank you. Thank you. I don't mean to be ungrateful. I'm just a little scared."

Joyce reached over and touched me on the shoulder. "It really looked like a Newfy. What did you mean Pippa said she'd be back?"

"I talked to an animal communicator. That's what Pippa told her to tell Elsa."

Joyce sighed, shook her head. She didn't need my craziness. There was too much serious work ahead of us in the real world.

"Make sure I get a copy of the cloud picture."

I had had one dog "bleed out" after delivering her puppies. As soon as they began nursing, she began hemorrhaging. A friend's dog simply died on the way home with the puppies. Blood clot, it was assumed. When we pulled into McDonald's for coffee, I pressed my thumb against Elsa's gums and watched as the skin turned pale and then bright pink again. She was fine, stable. At some point the anesthesia would wear off and she'd feel pain. Joy was fast asleep, curled up next to Elsa. Mamie sat up, hovering over the pups, moving them about, keeping them warm, cooling them off, unwrapping them, pulling some from corners where they were crowding and yelling. Some heads burrowed upwards and sniffed the air. They were very active, squealing and mewing, complaining. Were they too hot? Too cold? Hungry? Dave, driving steadily, assured me, "They'll be fine, just fine. Have a donut. Go to sleep. There won't be much sleep when you get home." Mamie groaned at the very concept of donut. Mamie told me later that she had been sick to her stomach in the back seat all the way home. It must have been a combination of being very tired and the oppressive heat in the car. Both Elsa and I lifted our heads when we turned through the gates of our home and up the bumpy driveway.

CHAPTER FOUR

It's a rocky road from concept to conception. There are no sign posts and no guarantees. When Elsa came into heat, we waited ten days, and then began a week of two hour road trips to Ithaca where we took progesterone readings and cytology tests every other day. Finally Elsa was getting ready to breed. Without the Cornell tests I would have known she was on her way as the boys had begun howling and stopped eating. They howled through the night. The boys can define that smell miles away. The coyotes knew about it and moved in closer. No matter where I jailed Elsa, the boys howled. They followed her scent in the grass, through the floor of the garage, three floors up in my bedroom. They were in agony. It was now all about scent. The boys were counting down the days as we were, but with far more exactitude. Our energy-saving trick was to take Elsa for a run around the trails. She marked her territory fastidiously, announcing her oncoming condition to all and everyone, including, I suspect, the timing, writing out her invitations in pungent urine every few feet. She was never alone as we stayed on watch for courting coyotes. The excursion finished, Elsa was put away and the boys would go out and take off, following her trail which they in turn marked, claimed, covering her scent with their scent. Inevitably Elsa's trail led right back to their kennels which saved us a lot of walking. A young boy who worked here with his mother, extrapolating from dogs to boys, asked his mother if, when he was ready for sex, would he have to smell the girls first. It wasn't fair to laugh.

And then her bloodwork said it was time to breed. We couldn't wait to use our Solomon, a huge, 160 pound, elegant, sweet, solemn dog with the most expressive of eyes. Solomon and Elsa travelled in separate crates to Cornell, Solomon whining and howling with desire as we drove the hour. I had one stud dog who, when he knew a girl was ready, would ignore her and jump in the car because he knew that going to Cornell was part of the process. First you get in the car, then this amazing thing happens. Solomon was up for amazing. At Cornell, he dragged my husband through the entry doors, took a right through the waiting room to the amusement of the other patients and the alarm of the waiting dogs, took a left, stopped to weigh in on the scale, headed down the hall, took a left, then a fast right, and skidded to a stop in front of the breeding room where he had been many times. He knew the course.

Oh how I wished to get Solomon's puppies. He is probably the best dog we've ever produced. He has an enormous bowling ball head with a saintly expression in his eyes and a sperm count in the billions. While most dogs do not make eye contact for more than a brief glance, Solomon lays his paw on your shoulder, holds you in place, and stares into your soul. Astonishing us all, he does this with visitors, staff, us, sometimes another dog. Solomon's mom, Celeste, came to us from Brittany, the results of a breeding between a girl I'd sent over and a major Swedish champion. Solomon was a champion. Elsa's sire and dam were champions. Elsa and Solomon's common grandmother won the amazing title of World Champion Veteran at eleven and half years. It was a worthy gene package. Being a champion implies soundness, a steady temperament, excellent movement, and beauty. His pedigree implied talent (his father had earned all the performance titles), agreeability, and longevity. Solomon is impressive. Above all, however, he is respectful. People want to talk to him. People with problems sit with him and absorb the sweet presence of power and kindness. One walker with romance problems would bring him back toward the house from his walk in the woods and sit on a bench under a willow tree, next to the hosta garden, bury her head in his neck and weep. Then, and only then, could she lead him down the hill to his indoor/outdoor run. When the next walker, who had lost his real job, began walking the dogs, Solomon would sit by the bench and wait for him to talk. Now, Solomon, no matter who is walking him, sits at the bench and, priest- like, waits patiently for the confession. He cannot be moved until someone talks to him for a few minutes. He becomes stone.

Once, up in Saskatchewan, I found a magnificent gothic carved walnut confessional booth in an antique shop. The shop owner suggested it could become a terrific commode, wild, sacrilegious, but terrific. Almost room size there was no way I could get it back to the states, no way I could afford it, but whenever I pass Solomon's garden bench, I imagine the confessional booth there, gleaming under the willow tree by the hosta garden with Solomon inside the cabinet, waiting to help whoever is troubled. Forgive me for switching religions, but, if anything, he is Buddha-like. I am here to help you. What do you need?

Choosing the correct father takes courage, sometimes blind courage. After all, traits aren't always overt. Genes lurk, waiting to combine with other genes. I've depended on the universe for this as well. You never know how the genes will fall, just like the dice in a crap shoot. I hate to "breed out" to a new kennel. You put two and two together, you could get five or seven unlikely lurking combinations of genes that have been waiting for decades to find each other. You can examine pedigrees just so far back but you never really know what's lurking or indeed, what a new combination will bring out. When Ishtar (from my first litter) had her litter of thirteen, eight of them had double rear dew claws. Newfies do not have rear dew claws. They have one up front above the ankle.

37

I called Kerry Brown. He laughed at me, asked me what I was drinking. Dew claws have to be removed at three days. I swore to him I had counted and had everyone around me count: eight double rear dew claws. He sighed. "Well, bring them in." I called Topmast Kennels. Yes, indeed. Margaret Wilmott who owned Topmast Kennels explained to me that during the First World War, (1914-1918), there were very few Newfies left in Europe. Were they eaten? Shot because there wasn't food for them? The few Newfies left were bred with the few Great Pyrenees left and those Great Pyrenees HAD DOUBLE REAR DEW CLAWS. Here was a gene waiting almost a hundred years to present itself. So we can all be clever and do all of our homework but there are secrets and surprises waiting in every breeding.

After years of breeding I know my own dogs'genetic faults fairly well. But there is always the unexpected. Choosing a stud is similar to choosing a puppy from a litter. You spend hours, cross-eyed, poring through the ancestral pedigrees, talking to other breeders, looking for gossip, experience, nastinesses, bad news. For example: that line bites people. That line has undescended testicles. That line has produced far too many torn cruciates. That line has cherry-eye (a tear gland in the eye that has to be stitched back into the socket). That line produces three kinds of heart problems. That breeder, I've heard, turns in the same excellent x-rays to the Orthopedic Foundation of America for evaluation each time. Same x-rays, different dog. So she claims excellent hips for all of her dogs whether good or not. That breeder's puppies lose the hair on their ears. That breeder shipped a blind puppy out. That male produced a litter of cleft palates (all had to be euthanized). And nightmare after nightmare. Add to that the crap shoot factor, and trusting in the universe factor, and the gossip factor -- you have the menu for deciding who breeds with whom. All puppies are cute. All breeders are not. It takes a long, long time to "see" a dog's potential, a long, long time to develop a network of other breeders who will trust you with their truths. Until, ultimately, choosing a pup or a stud becomes a matter of pure aesthetics: this dog, like a sculpture, works.

At any rate, I turned my trust to the Universe. With slender young women interns, residents, two professors, all rubber-gloved, on their knees, Solomon cooperated whole-heartedly until the grinning professor held up a victorious vial of milky fluid. Lesson over. Solomon was led from the room, looked over his shoulder at the assembled as if he had perhaps missed something, and walked back to the car. I'm not a great breeder, not a natural. When a dog stops to poop on the trail, I always turn my back to offer them privacy. Don't know if this is my weakness or being ridiculously polite, or anthropomorphizing or just the way I was brought up. Some things are private. You always close the bathroom door. Do dogs get embarrassed? Sex and bowel activity seem to require privacy. At least for me. Probably not for the dogs. Solomon being ejaculated in public embarrassed me as it always does, but I was so hungry for those puppies to happen. Everyone else in the room was matter-of-fact. One of the interns put the vial into her blouse, into her bra, and ran off to the lab to examine the quality and the count. We waited.

Billions. Elsa was inseminated with a long tube. I held her rear up so gravity would take its course as the billions swam toward the world of eggs and we retold our joke: why does it take a billion sperm to get a dog pregnant? Answer: because guys never ask directions. We tell it each time and everyone laughs politely each time. Probably heard it a lot already. After ten minutes of this awkward position, Elsa was set down on all fours, walked out with us, was not allowed to pee, into the car. Solomon started howling, but stopped very quickly. He and Elsa licked each other's noses through the fencing of their crates. It was over.

Why not let them mate naturally? The boys are so large and strong, I'm always afraid they'll hurt the girls or pull out their own shoulders, or ejaculate too early and lose the magic moment for breeding.

CHAPTER FIVE

A month after Elsa had been bred, it was time for her to go to Cornell where she would lie under the room-sized sonogram machine and have puppies counted, if indeed there were puppies. The ideal litter size is eight to ten puppies: one for each nipple, eight to ten being the usual nipple count. Judging from the size Elsa had already reached, eight to ten nipples would not be enough. In the meantime I spent my days prodding and poking Elsa for signs.

Initially, after breeding, the hormones kick in and the girl will stop eating for a day. That was not true this round. Elsa ate the day after breeding. In a few weeks you should be able to feel a swelling just past the ribs. That was true because she really started to eat and the swelling I felt could very well have been fat pockets and not the uterus. Then the mammary glands start to sprout. That's a good sign. The problem with all of these guessing game signs is that all the body changes happen whether or not the lady actually has puppies. Unlike human pregnancies, dog bodies can go through all the stages of pregnancy with or without puppies present. Some go as far as producing milk but no puppies. So no sign was significant except one: a crazy mystical sign, which proved nothing except that I was desperately willing to believe anything.

The sign: our home sits on a hill in such a way that the basement opens out to the lower level and the first floor to the higher level. The kennels are in the basement. A path runs alongside the house upwards to the front and then leads to open fields. I had taken my two grand old ladies -- Elsa's mother, Laalaa, and Elsa's grandmother Katie -- from their kennel and was walking them up the path, chatting with them. The air was brisk, clean, and fresh. I wore my sister's raccoon coat (she had moved to Florida). My ladies moseyed behind me, sniffing, reading their newspaper of grass. When we reached the top of the path, not ten feet from my house, I met a pair of foxes. They watched our approach from a triangular patch of weeds and snow, their great red winter coats drifting in the wind. A pair of foxes, one small, one large. I froze. Two foxes sat shoulder to shoulder looking at me. My God! Ten feet from me, looking directly at me, in daylight. What do you want? My neck felt as if someone were dropping beads of ice down my spine. Do you have a message? Maybe I didn't look like a raccoon. Maybe I looked like a giant gray fox.

My lady dogs were astonishingly unperturbed at the sight of the foxes. Did everyone but me know each other? Had I been left out of the visiting fox loop all these years? I swung around, grabbed the martingale collars on my two dogs and dragged/ran them back to their kennels. After I caught my breath, I raced upstairs to the first floor and looked out the window. The foxes were gone. What were they doing? What did they want? Why in the world were they presenting themselves to me, to the dogs? And why so serenely? In the daylight? Aren't they nocturnal? Don't they hibernate? And why didn't my old ladies react? In Japanese myth the fox is worshipped as a sacred creature who brings messages. In Port Crane, New York, they might also be rabid and/or carry the fatal leptospirosis disease. I made a mental note to call the vet and ask him what I should do. Call a trapper? Take a dog with me when I walked outside? I called the trapper. The trapper said that this was a good time to trap a fox because they have their winter coats on. I said I'd call him later to set up a date. I knew I wouldn't. Instead I gave them names. Vicky for the vixen, Sly for the male. I decided, then and there, that they had brought a message: my girl would indeed have puppies.

At last it was time for the sonogram. Praying had never made much difference and it seemed a selfish thing to bother God and/or the Universe. We drove the hour to Cornell Veterinary Hospital with Elsa. Because my dogs don't consider themselves dogs and take their behaviors from mine – which means following my example -- which means Elsa climbed into a chair in the waiting room and sat properly, behaving in the way I behaved, amusing all the other clients. Since most of the clients are there for end-game treatment, the good news of new life made everyone happy.

Bob and I marched Elsa down the prestigious halls to the sonogram room. I said, "Car," which extrapolates to get up and get in. Elsa hopped onto a chair and up onto the examining table. "Roll over, Elsa." She'd done this before: four times before with no good news. She knew the routine. Elsa rolled over on her back, lifted her legs in the air. (If you teach your dog one trick, "Roll over" should be at the top of the list in case of emergencies.) I placed a pile of towels under her head. They shaved her belly. We looked at a murky undulating mass of heart beats, breakfast, and black blobs. Elsa was extraordinarily pregnant. Cornell's sonogram system is ultimately reliable. It can measure the thumbnail- sized fetuses, count their heart beats. The doctor measured the blob heads to determine birth days. "At least ten," she announced phlegmatically. "November 23 give or take two days on either side." I watched the tiny hearts beating furiously. Mine was as well. We would have puppies.

Ten is a large litter. The Cornell sonogram doctor had said at least ten. At least ten is an even larger litter. And I suspected this litter would be large. Elsa's mom, Laalaa, had had fourteen pups; her grandma Katie thirteen, her great grandma Ishtar thirteen. We had one month to prepare. Forget Thanksgiving and company and family festivities. Forget Christmas. Actually forget the next four months until the pups were ready to go to their new homes. These pups were due give or take two days with Thanksgiving in the middle. We would have to think in terms of two litters, separate the litter in half. How will we identify one pup from the other? We'd have to divide the pups for nursing and bottle feeding. How will we separate the pups from each other? We would need to double our supplies of blankets, towels, baby wipes, bottles, formulas, thermometers, vitamins, and we needed to build a second whelping box so some could nurse with their mom and the others could be contained while we bottle-fed them ourselves. Our whelping boxes are six by six feet wide and three feet high. To prepare them, we lay down linoleum, add a single shelf inside the walls for the puppies to find protection from their mother if she rolls over onto them. In one of the walls, we cut a door opening with guillotine slats to contain the puppies. We needed lots of lumber. We needed a new digital scale. My old one – actually a beaten-up inherited infant scale – was missing a foot. Puppies slid around in it and often off it. Since we weigh puppies twice daily to see if they are getting enough to eat, using a digital scale would save lots of time and give us much greater accuracy. We had just heard a news report that heating milk in plastic bottles sent the toxins in the plastic into the formula. So we, as well as thousands of mothers of human babies, were scouring the internet at the same time for glass baby bottles. And with all the people we would have to hire and the energy I'd have to spend on puppy care, we needed easy food in the house. That meant three large frozen food orders in insulated containers from Omaha Steak, boxes which would also later serve perfectly for bringing the puppies home from the hospital. The list went on and on. Cases of Jiffy corn bread mix and boxes of liver from grass-fed cows for Elsa, probiotics for the mother and the infants. More blankets, more towels, baby wipes. More, more, more of everything. This was not going to be a simple project. It was an invasion.

CHAPTER SIX

With a few weeks to go, poor Elsa had been huge, spread, her breasts skimming along the floor as she waddled, leaving snail trails of milk on the wood. I knew in my bones that Elsa was worried as well. Actually, I believe she was frightened because of the changes coming in her. When her grandmother Ishtar was dying...she could no longer stand or walk...we would lift her up and help her outside to urinate. She would never go out unless both Bob and I were with her. No one else would do. If someone else were helping her, she'd stop, freeze, look over her shoulder for whichever one of us was missing. I realized how frightened she was that she had lost her abilities. We sense our dogs' emotions. A worried dog is lethargic, without appetite, clingy, just different, and depressed. It shows. Our pregnant Elsa, normally a happy tail-wagger, was depressed. She must have been terrified. What's happening to me? I can't move. I can't run. I feel awful. I can't protect myself. I can't protect my people. She might have been in pain. She had lost her power, her ease of movement, her strength.

I would wake up in the mornings with fear in my legs as I thought about the mass of puppies. If I was nervous Elsa probably was as well. She clung to me, cried if I left her in her kennel. How much could she understand? I had to speak with Elsa, to reassure her, to explain these things that were happening to her.

Looking for guidance, I called Mary Long, the animal communicator. Crazy as it may be, I hear "messages" through her from my dogs, living and dead, in something like an etheric conference call. Sometimes the messages make me happy, sometimes they inform me, and sometimes they knock my socks off. Even if they aren't true, they make me happy.

Mary Long calls herself an animal communicator and that's exactly what she does. Or she has a terrific imagination, which, since imagination is my bailiwick, she doesn't. When Mary and her sister were children they thought everyone could talk with animals. As soon as they started kindergarten, they discovered otherwise. I call Mary on the phone, describe in a few details the dog I want to have a conversation with. She contacts the dog after I describe it. She hears and sees the dog and somehow "connects" to it. There are many animal communicators now. The word they use for talking to dogs is 'channeling'.

Mary Long has been channeling my dogs for ten years. She knows my dogs, those who are alive as well as those who have died. I call Mary when death is imminent, when there is a difficult to diagnose illness, prior to surgery, during competition, ("Joey, for Godsakes, you're in the show ring. Hold your head up higher.") when there are behavior problems, food issues, or when I am painfully lonely for a dog who has died. I lean heavily on Mary Long,

Mary has a PhD in math with an emphasis on entropy: no small mind this one. Retiring after a thirty- year career as a mathematician at Dupont Chemical, she began to talk with small audiences to build up a clientele who wanted to communicate with their pets. Math, not creative imagination, is Mary Long's high card. When she "reports" something funny -- for example a cat who told her she can't wait to get to heaven so she can have a cigarette -- she laughs in surprise just as I do, just as if she is also hearing that something for the first time. She is often astonished by what she hears. When my lovely girl Ishtar told her that Newfoundlands are from the star Sirius where they were very small, close to the ground, and they came down to earth to help humans, Mary and I were dumbfounded. I'm the writer. I'm the one who makes things ups. That being said, I can assure the reader that I could not have myself made up any of these bizarre, often illogical, and unexpected conversations.

And certainly, trained in advanced mathematics, Mary Long was less capable than I at wild flings of imagination and utter silliness. Whatever Mary Long does, it works for me. True or not, the emotion of the conversations was oddly accurate and often so skewed, the details seemed impossible to make up. Once Mary allowed herself to contact my dead mother; my mother and I then continued our earthly argument about her third husband until I was frightened and hung up.

Sometimes Mary and I don't use the phone. She's visited here; I've visited at her horse farm in Delaware. Our Elsa's uncle Joey was showing near Mary's horse farm one weekend. Mary came to the show grounds to cheer him on. She had not been to a dog show before and knew very little about the routine and the requirements of showing well. Joey told her, "I'm going to make believe I'm swimming. I'm going to hold my head high out of the water, stretch my front legs as far as they can go, and kick my rear legs as hard as I can. Also my handler isn't the top handler anymore." His handler had been the top and now was really slowing down. I had never connected the swimming mode with the running mode. Joey did. He looked beautiful and powerful and took the points that day. Later we all went to an outdoor upscale sandwich shop and ordered turkey batards. We didn't know what a batard was. Turned out to be a French word for a small roll as opposed to a loaf: a little bastard. Two mutts sat with their owner at a table next to us, watching hungrily as every mouthful disappeared. Mary laughed, reported their words. "We like batards too," the dogs had said to her. "We speak French."

The one message that convinced my husband of the authenticity of these psychic connections was a message from Lulu. Our Lulu, whom we privately called Woo Woo, spoke to us through Mary Long. "I want to say something and I know I'm saying it wrong but I want to say it this way anyway. I wuv you." There was no way anyone could have known that we called her Woo Woo. It was exactly what Lulu would have said if she talked. Or had she? Or, now passed on, does she?

There's plenty of proof that Mary Long knows things she couldn't possibly know unless she is acting telepathically, non-locally. Sometimes I hear nothing convincing, lots of generic conversation that could apply to any dog, but most times I hear absolutely indisputable spot-on information. The factual proof is not the real proof. The real proof is in the precision of the emotional responses, individualized and familiar. I wuv you. There was no way Mary Long could have known that.

The first thing Elsa said to Mary Long was, "I don't think I can fit through doors anymore. Will they cut me open?" The second question was, "Will they put me together again?"

That's when Pippa, a great great aunt, long-gone, entered the conversation and promised to come back to help.

Because Elsa had developed a more human, less instinctual fabric, I suspected she would be a terrible mother. Just as I had been. Her great grandmother Ishtar, when she had her thirteen puppies, took one look at the squirming mewing mass, turned her back -- which I easily interpreted as, "Forget it, Mom. This was your idea, not mine"-- and we did all the cleaning and feeding, every hour on the hour for weeks. At the most she would lie still while they suckled. There was going to be a lot of work and I doubted Elsa would help. So intensely, exquisitely attuned as she had become to our emotions, our actions and reactions, our habits, our words, the very fabric of our lives. (Mom's putting on makeup which means she's going someplace in the car. Quick, get a shoe so I can go too.) I doubted she could leave her acquired nature behind in order to accommodate motherhood as a dog. Unfortunately I was right.

In varying degrees, our companion dogs seem to have a double nature: the wild and the domesticated. It has to be a struggle for them to adapt to our needs, our demands, and their own dog natures. I wonder if it's an uneasy, bewildering mix. I know there's a continuum. Some of the dogs are wilder, more natural than others. The ones who are more human or humanized are more neurotic, perhaps more connected to our neuroses. This was not true of Celeste, Elsa's aunt. Comparing Celeste with Elsa helped me to see Elsa more clearly.

Celeste had every dog instinct: difficult to live with, independent, great to live with, taking off and running-away (I was just going swimming. You knew I'd be back). She was all dog, with a strong trace of the wild. We never knew what she would do next. She and her brother Theo, Elsa's father, were the first pups to come live with us that we hadn't bred and raised. Celeste is not quite attached, not quite dedicated. If a storm is coming on and I'm taking dogs for a walk, Celeste won't stay with me but she will stop at the barn and wait for me to return. Other dogs, more attached, would cross in front of me, stop me, step on my feet, or pull at my sleeve. It's the bit of wildness left in her. Or perhaps not. Perhaps she is signaling me to go no further. When she stands on the slate hill above the barn, outlined in the moonlight, wolf-like, a huntress ready to pounce, I admit being afraid of that which is wild in her. When she meets me outside, she races toward me and then, touching my hand, walks beside me. She is a mysterious girl, but good as gold. I remember how she would spring away from my touch when she didn't want to go into her kennel. But she always waited for me, torn between running away and coming home. Being a kenneled dog did not come easily to her. Before she had pups I tried to sleep with her in my bed. She was restless. Not a house dog. We have one hundred and forty acres. When

Celeste would find herself unattended, free, she would take off. The moment Elsa would find herself free she would dash upstairs and bury herself in the comforter on my bed. Not Celeste. On the coldest of nights, if I didn't shut the guillotine separating her outside run from her inside run, Celeste would curl up on a wooden palette outside, much preferring the arctic temperatures. Sometimes we closed the guillotines and left her outside by error. In the morning, covered with snow, she'd shake off and come back inside. No problem. I'm an arctic dog. When I brought her food bowl to her indoor kennel, she would pop her big handsome head through the plastic strips from outside, asking me to let her eat al fresco. I pushed her bowl into the outdoor run. A wild dog, a wild and wonderful dog, a creature of instinct.

Celeste and Elsa are so unalike. Celeste, wild and willful. Elsa, willing and human. When Celeste had her litter of ten, she did all the work.

CHAPTER SEVEN

Elsa's puppies were still only a few hours old when we at last pulled in through the gates. They were frantic with their first experience of hunger. Elsa whimpered as we hit the potholes in my driveway, lifted her head, hurting, I'm certain. Tears ran down my face. Relief? Joy? Everything. I had to see Bob. I had to show him what I'd done as if I had done it. I was so proud. Elsa couldn't have cared less. No proud mother she. We set up her ramp and maneuvered her as gently as possible from the car to the ground. I waited while she made a long, long pee in the garden. In the snow around Elsa I noticed paw prints, too large for a cat, too small for a coyote, thought the foxes might have returned. "We have to keep an eye out for foxes, Mamie. They carry lots of diseases." And messages, I reminded myself. Bob kissed me on both cheeks as if he were giving me a medal, pointed out a lacework of fox prints in the snow, then peeked into the Omaha Steak box, and grinned. Joy. Elsa finished her squat and headed toward the house, collapsed on the coolness of the kitchen floor. I offered her a bowl of cold water. She turned her head away. What have you done to me? I couldn't help her.

Once Elsa was settled in the basement office – a fireplace, two sleeping sofas, two easy chairs, shelves, a small kitchen, and a huge desk for our nursery equipment -- we brought the precious Omaha Steak boxes in. The office was warm and ready. The three thermometers showed 85. Bob had followed instructions to the T. Everything was ready: towels, blankets, the digital scale I had splurged on, food for Elsa, formula in the dogs' basement kitchen, sterilized bottles, two generators waiting just beyond the doors, bottles of Pedialyte, cans of condensed milk, bottles of Karo Syrup (in case we had to mix our own formula) antibiotics, intravenous set-ups, baby vitamins, fresh clothing, pale blue piles of surgical scrubs, bottles of disinfectant, hand sanitizers, balls of wool of every color, and new fleecy socks for anyone who came into the house, and four dozen containers of grooming wipes a friend of my daughter's had mailed from Los Angeles (Our news was spreading along the Internet. There were videos of the incubator party on You Tube.) And then there was Elsa's grandmother Katie, waiting for us, sniffing puppy air. She knew what was coming. Katie always knew what was coming.

Next to the basement office there is a kitchen which was once an operating room installed by the psychiatrist who built the house originally. The doctor ran the state mental hospital and did, I heard from the people who removed the operating table, the illegal and necessary abortions here in the basement. So, conveniently, we had water, electricity, heat, air-conditioning, sink, shelves, and good lighting. Katie, Elsa's grandmother, waited in the office. She knew what was coming. She sniffed puppy air and she wanted to be part of the mothering. Or take over. At thirteen, having had two great litters herself, Katie lay outside the office desperate to get to the puppies. I didn't know if Elsa would take offense and decide to protect her puppies. We found a puppy gate Katie could look through but not get through. It wasn't enough. She continued to nose the gate down until we secured it with bungee cords. Katie was frantic to get in. I think puppies arouse hormonal activity in other females. Litters ago, a young woman with two children came to help me with a litter of pups. She not only began her period two weeks early but started producing milk. So Katie may have indeed been turned on, unlike Elsa with her negligent hormones. Actually I didn't think Elsa would care if Katie came in and took all the puppies. She had yet to pay any attention to them. Did she even know they were her "things"?

We divided the litter in half; put eight in one whelping box and nine in the other. Elsa refused to go into the whelping box. The pups had gone two hours without feeding. The two preemie girls absolutely had to be fed. We coaxed and pulled and pushed. Having most recently escaped the confinement of the womb to discover the astonishing and sublime joys of warm bottles of milk and the safety of the Omaha Steak box, the pups abandoned in the second whelping box were now miserably deprived of all, and howled unremittingly. The howling alarmed Elsa. She turned into concrete and balked. I hated to force her but I had to take her by the collar and drag her in with the puppies, a dangerous moment at that. Once the necessity or my power was established, she lay down, rolled over, and sighed. We held her in place and attached pups to her nipples. I don't think she was cooperating. I think she was just too weak to refuse. "Good girl," we said, over and over again." Good girl." It was ninety degrees in the whelping box. Sixtyfive degrees is the upper safe limit for these arctic dogs. Elsa's tongue hung out. She panted heavily. I lifted her head to syringe cool water into her mouth. She would not look at me. When you have dogs who live to look in your eyes, who drink your very soul, the turn of the head is crushing. I don't want to see you.

Some pups fell off. Some pups prefer the lower nipples, some the ones closest to the head. So we shifted them back and forth. Elsa's breasts were enormous. It wasn't easy for the tiny mouths to encompass the nipples. We dabbed honey on the nipples to attract the puppies. Except for smell, touch, and temperature, as far as I know, they had no senses working. I'm not sure about taste. The honey worked. Elsa looked over her shoulder once or twice to see what the dickens was going on, what were those dreadful things, what were they doing on her body, but she was too tired to fight or even move away. I tried to remember what it felt like when my first baby suckled. Peculiar, half-sexual, half-something indefinable, intimate enough to be embarrassing. I didn't enjoy it. Or I was afraid to enjoy it. In fact, my mother poked her head in the doorway once, shook her head, and declared, "Barbaric", and I switched to feeding my own baby with a bottle. Whatever I brought to breeding puppies did not come from my own mothering experience. Like Elsa, I wasn't a natural either.

Eventually, although it was a long frustrating process, we had eight suckling, Elsa lying still, eyes closed, the puppies neatly lined up at her large belly, working, heads nodding in unison, pumping Elsa's swollen belly with their front feet, their little tails up in the air, their tips curled downward – a sign that they are getting milk. They looked so much like furry mini oil pumps across the vast, rich white tundra of Elsa's belly. Well, the metaphor dies. Not so rich. She had very little milk. I heated water, mixed the powder, filled the baby bottle, found a tiny preemie nipple. Wrapped in a washcloth, a velvety mole of a puppy, one of the preemie girls, curled in my hand, pressed against my breast. I touched her mouth with the nipple of the baby bottle, squeezed a few drops into her incredibly perfect mouth. Somehow, miraculously, amazingly, she got it. She latched onto the nipple and suckled and drank the milk. I felt her belly filling. Thank God. Because Elsa was producing very little milk, there were sixteen more that had to be fed. We filled more bottles. By the time the pups were fed, cleaned, stimulated to poop and pee, it was time to start over again.

Joy shooed us out of the whelping box and took over the puppies. Her meds had worn off. We pulled the other half of Elsa's puppies from the second whelping box, two at a time, and bottle-fed their ferocious little selves. Then we stimulated their bottoms just under the pelvic bone, and cheered when they pooped a strange, seeded mustardy poop, which was normal. As soon as the second team was fed and cleaned, we put them in the whelping box with Elsa and took the others out. The second shift nursed under Joy's guidance while Mamie and I bottle-fed the first set, burped them by patting them on their backs, wiped them clean, rubbed their bottoms until they evacuated one element or another. Each contribution resulted in an announcement from us, a happy, competitive announcement. "Mine pooped. Look at that. Wow, look at mine." Our consciousness was entirely focused on input, output, and weight. Some of the puppies didn't cooperate easily and took much too long, which worried me. It might mean the formula was too thick. I would add more water. Was something wrong with the powder itself in the formula? I had once had a litter on prepared formula who didn't evacuate. Another breeder, who herself had had seven children, told me when the mother's milk is really healthy, everything is absorbed and you never see poop. Her own seven human children rarely pooped when they were still nursing. That was news but not enough to calm my paranoia. A friend who had a litter at the same time I had, using the same formula from the same manufacturer's batch, lost all of her puppies in a few days. I just worried sooner and was able to save my pups before their bowels became totally blocked and their systems septic. I put the warning on the internet immediately. The manufacturer called and berated me for putting it on the internet before I contacted him. Something in the formula was not being absorbed correctly. I felt no sympathy for him.

When all of the puppies had suckled with tidal force on Elsa (as well as our noses and fingers and each other) and all had been fed, we led Elsa out of the whelping box. She collapsed at our feet, drank a few sips of water. I held Mr. Yellow to Elsa's nose. "Look, sweetheart. This is Mr. Yellow. Look. It's your puppy." Elsa turned her head away. Elsa had no interest in licking her pups to move their bowels or open their bladders, no interest in cleaning them up afterward, no interest at all. And worst of all, no interest in me. I flopped on one of the beds. Mamie and Joy weighed the puppies, filled in the blanks on the forms Bob had printed up for us: the amount of fluid they'd taken, the evacuation report (who pooped, who didn't), the weights, wrote comments into a notebook. "Red puppy crying. Blue-green puppy didn't poop. Need Cream for our coffee. Prefer Hazelnut half and half. More fox prints around the house, right next to the kennels and up at the barn."

I knelt beside the plank side of the whelping box. Seventeen new-born Newfoundlands crept across a field of fleece, exploring. The fleece was pink from the red glare off the heat lamps over the puppies: seventeen fragile lives just arrived from nothingness, utterly dependent. Deaf, blind, sprung into gravity without ceremony from the warmth, safety, and endless plenty of their uterine weightlessness, they sought desperately milk and warmth, determined to survive. And Elsa's nipples were on empty. The pups suckled until they fell off the nipples in exhaustion but their bellies were flat and soft. There was no milk.

This lady daydreamer who leaves the milk bottle in the microwave, gets lost 90% of the time she's on the road…in her hometown…forgets to close the refrigerator door, and worse, now had to reach beyond herself, to do something, to be something greater than herself, to pay attention to absolutely every blood- red warning detail, to anticipate every fatal error, to be there and present for every breath, every twitch, every poop, every germ, every hiccup. I was banking on help from the universe. I was going to need all the help I could get. I felt, somehow, both stupid and chosen.

CHAPTER EIGHT

And so it began. That first night was bitterly cold. Northern winds whipped around our hill-top house. Trees snapped out in the woods, death snaps, gunfire cracks and crashes. Snow melt had turned to ice leaving treacherous paths. Our indoor-outdoor kennel runs are in the basement of our house. Wooden guillotine doors drop down between indoors and outdoors. The cracks and spaces in the doors were stuffed with hand towels against the cold. Blankets were piled high. The Newfies coupled in their runs slept close to each other. Terrified that we'd lose our power and the heat the puppies absolutely needed to survive, I checked the generators endlessly. Now and then coyote screams and yips punctuated the winds. My dogs, a good dozen of them – Newfoundlands all -- would wake from their sleeps, and answer their ancestors in one shuddering primal song. Since Thanksgiving was on its leftover way out, Christmas music filled the airways. Mamie turned on the radio every time she came into the room. I turned it off every time she left. It wasn't the music that threw me into Bah Humbug, it was the ever-frantic jabbering disc jockeys invading my head. Finally, I gave up. *Feliz Navidad* seemed to play every other tune. I couldn't get it out of my head. I couldn't stop humming it. Merry Christmas in Spanish? Happy birthday? Certainly happy birthday times seventeen.

It was not *Feliz Navidad* in our house that night. It was a night of fear. There was another sound that night, a cross between what I imagined would be the scream of a banshee and chalk on the blackboard. It was a vixen scream which scraped up and down my spine. The fox. Would she sneak in and steal a puppy? Eat a puppy? Or was it the fox with a message, just checking in. Congrats on your new babies. Or was it just a vagrant screech owl? No, I knew it was the fox. The dogs woke up and barked wildly at the sound. I shuddered with cold, with exhaustion, with fear. I suddenly remembered that the heat lamps should be covered with aluminum foil. How could I have forgotten such an important detail? What else have I forgotten? How else might I endanger these babies? We can't forget to give extra feedings to the little girls. I worked each nipple. They were virtually empty, just dribbles, not spurts. The puppies mewed with hunger. But Elsa had so little milk and the puppies' lives hung on such a thin thread. And I held that thread.

Elsa wouldn't make eye contact with me. She was overwhelmed, confused, drugged from her surgery, exhausted, hurting, and too hot to stay under the heat lamps. She retreated into a corner on cool tile, wrapped her great black and white silken self around herself, and, dead asleep, snored heavily, and left me in charge. Elsa was of little use. Mamie reminded me again and again that her little Malteses delivered their puppies under the bed, cared for them there, bothered no one. Not so in my house. I would have to supervise everything. In a few days, we promised each other, Elsa should produce wonderful milk filled with antibiotics of her own, warm and rich. In a few days she should be cleaning her pups, licking them, caring for them. But in the meantime we had to work twenty-four hours a day. Elsa would not eat, which meant she could produce no milk. She would not so much as lick her puppies' noses and certainly not their rears to stimulate evacuation. And she would not let me leave the room. If she were in the box nursing with Joy and Mamie holding her in place and I were to leave the room, she threw herself away from them, wrestled, and followed me while Joy and Mamie wildly gathered the puppies out of the way of Elsa's feet.

Under the heat lamps Elsa was miserably warm, panting, drooling, her tongue out a good three inches. Outside the whelping box, the rest of the room was still too warm for Elsa. 65 degrees is a good temperature for an arctic dog with a double fur coat. I couldn't help her. The heat lamps brought the temperature in the room itself up to 80. The pups' temperature had to be kept close to their mother's pre-birth uterine temperature of 102. The three thermometers in different areas near the boxes now read 90 degrees and that was enough. If the wind were to knock out the electricity, we had generators standing by. Enough, just enough to keep the heat lamps going over the whelping boxes. The neo-natal pups, the size and look of moles, had no way to control the heat of their bodies. One rush of cold air could chill and kill. When they were too cold they formed their slime mold mass, just as they had in the incubator in those first moments. When they were too warm they spread out and separated from each other. I did not know how, nor could I imagine how I could heat their formulas if the power went out. I thought about the possibility of tucking them all back into the Omaha Steak boxes and into the car. I wondered if I could heat water under the hood of the car. It was endlessly demanding to fight cold and heat and keep everything in balance: puppies warm, Elsa cool, the three sleep-deprived humans awake.

I picked up Mr. Dark Blue and held him against my cheek. I could feel his gentle breath. Over the years, in the midst of other puppy dramas and traumas, as Bob dragged dirty blankets to the washing machine and I scraped up poop, he would look at me and ask, "Why are we DOING this?" And we both would smile at each other because we knew why. I can't help myself. Anything so beautiful, so mysterious, so noble...one isn't enough. Like potato chips. I jokingly explain that anything worth doing is worth overdoing. Or that I am driven by curiosity. No, it is deeper than that. As I age, and I have considerably aged, and face mortality, to touch, to be touched by new life, is a great gift. My mother used to tell me that Mahatma Gandhi slept next to (she would explain no further) young girls to acquire their energy. It might be what I'm doing: dabbling in the eternal energy of life. While my future recedes, my ailments stalking me with their shovels on their shoulders, and even as these new puppies will age and die, there is still that brilliant moment, that moment when they arrive from the womb and I hold them in my hands, that moment when I am assured about one thing: life itself goes on and on even as I will not. I held a new-born puppy in my hand. I had brought them into the world. It was my duty to keep them there, whatever the labor, whatever the cost. The puppy nuzzled into my fingers seeking warmth and milk. I put him on Elsa's swollen nipple, and somehow –which always amazes me – he went to work. I wondered what else he knew, what anciently wired knowledge he had brought with him, what he might tell me.

Newfoundlands are old souls. They are treasures. And they are luxuries. They are the modern descendants of the Tibetan Mastiffs. Recently, a Tibetan Mastiff sold for a half million dollars plus. The news photo of his face was identical to my Theo's face, the grandfather of the seventeen puppies. The Tibetan dogs are the Newfoundland ancestors. Highly prized as companions and guard dogs for royalty as far back as l000 B.C., the antique Tibetan Mastiffs were known to give spiritual balance. No less than Genghis Khan and the Buddha are cited as owners. I know my Newfs are connected to something spiritual. Just as any good Buddhist, my dogs stand in front of me, look deep into my eyes and, I am quite certain, say, "I'm here. How can I help you?" The Mastiffs' tails curl up behind them. The pricey pure bred Mastiff purchased in China for such a vast sum had a black head, black body, brown legs and a curling tail. Once in a while Newf breeders will have a pup with a tail curling up and/or brown legs: both antique genes. The modern Newfy does lend spiritual balance: ask any Newfy owner. The antique Mastiff -- many mutt varieties of whom I met unpleasantly in Tibet -- is fiercely protective, even aggressive, more warrior. Today's Newfies are gentle, adoring, powerful, with excellent judgment. They have sweet expressions and loving eyes, a long flowing coat, and a huge, round head. The modern Newfy's superb judgment has replaced the Mastiff's guard dog aggression. After the many thousands of years living with humans, the Newfy's basic instinct -- basic *natural encoded* instinct – is to save our lives. Where does such a creature come from? What a gift to live with a powerful animal whose work is to save our lives. My favorite character tale is the Newfy who, when attacked at riverside by a pit bull, walked into the water with the pit bull clamped onto his neck until the pit bull drowned. That is wisdom beyond the norm. The puppies in our home that first night carried ancient noble blood, had the potential of greatness, kindness, and wisdom: souls. I could not feel more responsibility. I had brought them into the world, through my decision, and it was up to me to defend them from error, illness, cold, hunger, accident, stupidity, laziness. They were my burden and a terrible burden it was. I couldn't wait until they looked into my eyes and showed me the blossom of their souls.

I lay on one of two sofa beds watching puppies. Mamie, lay on the other. Joy was in the whelping box with the puppies. The coyotes and my dogs howled in their timeless responsive measures. The disc jockeys and I were pretty much stuck on *Feliz Navidad* and *O Holy Night*.

Mamie slipped into a silvery ski jacket, wrapped a blanket over her shoulders, and led Elsa outside. Elsa went dutifully, grateful, I'm sure, to escape the oppressive heat of the puppy's room and to be doing something familiar, something she at least understood. I followed Elsa and Mamie outside, gave Mamie a flashlight, and turned on the barn lights.

Moonlight streamed across the snowy fields. I tossed kibble around my feet in case the fox returned. Great gusts of wind swept clouds across the face of the moon -- moon birds. I asked the stars to take notice of the puppies, to grant them long lives. "And me too," I added just in case any one/thing/ being/ idea was listening. "Take notice of me and guide me through this. Let them all be healthy. Let me understand and help Elsa and know how to take care of her puppies for her. Help me to be as strong and unafraid as Elsa, at least as Elsa should be." The sky was so much larger than I was, so much larger than the puppies. "Do you think we're small and unimportant, Mamie, or we're connected to the sky? Do you think the sky sees us? Are the stars narrowing their gaze, watching us?"

I asked Mamie if she thought we could concentrate on one of the stars, say that one in the Big Dipper, did she think we could win the lottery or save a puppy's life? She said I sounded mental. I am mental as opposed to physical. But she meant crazy. She shook her head, took Elsa's lead, and walked into the dark. I imagined her grumbling to herself about me and concluding that a job is a job. Even though her eyes twinkle, I'd caught the edge of a grim mouth. I would try not to burden her with my far-flung sleep-deprived imagination. "Do you think," I said to her back, "Do you think that there's some power up there we've forgotten? Do you think the stars are playing with us? That we're their puppets and they're pulling our destinies on strings, making us dance the dance of life and death down here?" I thought so. And now and then, I went on to myself, are we able to offer a faint tug upward on our puppet strings (call it prayer) and take a few steps of our own? Beat them at their own game? I was, after all, a newcomer, dabbling in creation. And that, I have decided, is what draws me to this drama when I could be playing Mahjong and picking out chocolate covered raisins from the bridge mix.

When Mamie and Elsa materialized under the barn lights: from shadow to shape to person, Joy, wrapped in blankets, joined Mamie outside. I, from inside, watched the red tip of Joy's cigarette. I thought she was twenty or less. I found out she was thirty and had already lived too many destructive lives, on the street and in mental wards. She had spent the early hours of that first night in my house upstairs in a guest bedroom, then came down to the basement, and curled up on one of the sofa beds. Except to stash snacks under the bed in her new bedroom, she never slept there again. She needed to be with Mamie.

While the two women were outside with Elsa, I knelt again beside the box. The pups were red and pink in the light of the heat lamps, spread out, motionless. Then a twitch, then another, then they all twitched. It was as if an electric charge started with one and passed into the others, one after the other. Or a magic wand passed over them. Twitching is a good sign: their nerves are activating. They were growing. They fit in our hands. In a year or less they'd be over one hundred pounds. I touched each one. "We're going to win this game, puppies. You're all going to make it." And then something happened to me, something in my body moved toward them, something just below my ribs moved out toward the puppies, a transfer of an energy I had never felt before. It was something like sexual, an alertness, a draining out, but not. It was something about chakras and powers, about bonding, a transfer of energy from me to them. I didn't understand what happened to me and if indeed it had happened to them or if it happened to me from them. I didn't have time or the training to dwell on why or what. I knew it was a life-changing experience.

CHAPTER NINE

The beginning of Day Two. There were another few minutes before the six a.m. feeding. The puppies were a day old. I was a hundred years old. We were feeding the pups every two hours, the two little girls every hour.

After the early morning feedings, a sliver of daylight expanding from the east, I wrapped up in my sister's huge raccoon coat, put on my boots, grabbed a flashlight, and took a break for fresh air to wake me up. I inherited my sister's coat. Perhaps I looked like a giant raccoon, or better yet, really did smell like one. Perhaps I carried the waft of Elsa's afterbirth smells or the puppy smells. I took Solomon with me. After all, the night belongs to the wild ones and being alone in what was left of the night, even in animal disguise, I was, if not frightened, wary. A possum, ghostlike pale and prehensile crossed in front of me, I screamed and jumped five feet. Solomon chased him into the woods.

When it was already light enough to see clearly, I saw the fox, a fox. Vicky? I had no idea. Whoever it was, and I wanted to think it was she, Vicky poked her head out from behind the barn and watched as Solomon and I approached very slowly toward the barn. Her mate, whom we hadn't seen since they first appeared sitting next to the house, wasn't with her. Now I could see her full beautiful little body. "Vicky," I spoke out loud. She didn't react. She sat still and watched Solomon intently. "Hey, Vicky, do you think I'm a monster raccoon?"

My voice didn't frighten her. Had she heard it before? For how many years? Solomon was relieving himself, ripping up frozen grass, unaware or ignoring her. "If you were frightened, Vicky Vixen, wouldn't you disappear behind the barn? I know where your path is. I've seen just the white tip of your luxurious tail as it vanishes behind the barn, through a narrow space in the fencing, down the hill to one of your burrows. I know where you've been but never where you will be. Your footprints in the snow give you away. At night you visit the dog runs, around the barn, around the kennels, up to our front door, up the hill in front of house and then back in a great curve to your burrow place. You live underneath the shed, don't you? The dogs think so. They always visit there, sniffing and pawing. But you aren't frightened, are you? You are curious. I am also. Do you think we could be friends? You, your ancestors, have probably been on this land for generations. My animals like me. Could you like me? We just had puppies." A proper wild creature would have vanished at the first sound of my voice.

Vicky trotted half way down the hill toward Solomon, sat a bit of a distance from us, wagged her tail, inviting him. Holy Hannah! Solomon continued to sniff the ground. Impatiently, Vicky trotted further down the hill to us, ran around Solomon's legs until he looked over his shoulder at me, and then took off with her in wild chase. The two of them ran in exalted circles, appearing and disappearing. I was astonished that she would come so close to me. Have you chosen him for your new mate? He too has a gorgeous white tail.

Another dog barked from the kennels – deep-voiced Theo. Vicky turned and trotted away. Solomon came back to me, leaned heavily against me, panting. "How long has this been going on, Solomon?"

Is this how it happened with dogs and people so many thousands of years ago? Watching us, learning us, following us, taking our food when we toss it behind us, finally trusting us, and, at last, playing with us? Is this something – this possible friendship – our foxes will pass on to their fox children for generations and generations? Until one evening, some cold winter evening, one of them will be waiting at the front door, waiting to cross the threshold and come inside with everyone else and be one with us.

Later that day, I took big, black Theo out with me to look for Vicky. We followed her dainty tracks into a paddock. She leaped out of a dog house, flew over the fence, and away. It was Solomon she loved.

Midday of day two, wearing the raccoon coat over my nightgown, I walked the quarter mile driveway down to the mailbox to get the morning's paper and shake the sleep from my bones. I saw the fox from the corner of my next to me, moving alongside me, just a foot or so into the fir trees, just a flash of form and movement. I didn't have the feeling she was stalking me. I thought rather she was joining me, that large and oddly upright raccoon that I was out at dawn. *Her* coat was deep red, her tail magnificent. Was this Solomon's Vicky? She looked larger than she had, almost German shepherd size. Maybe the animal world was inviting me in. She didn't follow me back to the house. Was she dangerous? Rabid?

As if she were bringing me good fortune, the next morning and thereafter, now and then, the fox or a fox would follow me down the driveway and then disappear. I so wanted to think she was bringing me good fortune instead of rabies. But I loved her being with me. I tried not to read too much into her friendship. Of course, I did. "I am here," she said, I imagined, "to help you. I bring blessings and messages." Her tiny footprints surrounded the kennel gates, led up to the door of the whelping box room, back to the barn, down to the mailbox, once at the front door. Closer and closer. What was she thinking? Approaching a human being?

I decided the fox who followed me had to be Solomon's Vicky, Vicky with a great winter coat.

Often, but never often enough, Vicky followed us – a flash of reddish orange, a sense of presence from the corner of my eye, and then gone as soon as we turned. She remained behind, slid into the trees now and then, and, at the bottom of the driveway, veered away to take her own path down to the pond. Her footsteps were almost within ours, light, delicate, graceful little being that she was, making her way toward our lives, our Otherness.

CHAPTER TEN

At birth, most of Elsa's pups had weighed in at one pound plus a few ounces. The largest was Mr. Yellow who weighed almost two pounds; the smallest two girls, bird-like small, weighed under a pound. We prayed for the two preemie girls with thin bird bones and little flesh still struggling to survive. Through the night they had been fed every hour on the hour. They weren't sickly or malformed. They just hadn't been able to get enough food in the womb. They were not runts. And they weren't really preemies as they had all been born together. Usually the mother has three breedings. It's possible that these little girls were bred three days later than the rest of the litter and are therefore three days younger, not in time but in development. I know one excellent breeder who was surprised to hear this and admitted to letting the runts "go" because there must be something wrong with them. No, there was nothing wrong. They simply have to be fed smaller amounts (smaller stomachs) more often. There may not be such a thing as runts but there are such things as lazy breeders. And there are other breeders out there who leave mom and pups in the barn and count what's left every morning. The worst tale I've heard was from a young man who had worked in one of those notorious Amish puppy mills in Lancaster, Pennsylvania. He reported they simply tossed out buckets of dead and failing puppies. We had heard about a Newfy who had given birth to eighteen puppies but the puppies were the size of mice and all had died. We were very lucky. While she was carrying her pups, Elsa's body had supplied and supported all seventeen. Then it became my turn.

By the first morning weigh-in, we found that almost all of the pups had lost an ounce or two since weighing in at the hospital. The post-delivery weight loss is normal but always bears watching. Since the puppies were being fed every two hours, the two tiny preemies every hour on the hour, it took two hours to complete the feeding, the stimulating of the bladders and the bowels and then the cleaning. There wasn't any time to sleep. We hoped Elsa's hormones would kick in soon, that she'd then start to care for the puppies herself the way Celeste had. Often after a C-section the instinctual process of motherhood is delayed a few days, most likely because of the anesthesia and/or the system shock. She's supposed to roll them over, lick them clean, lick their bottoms until they evacuate, then clean them up again. This is what Celeste had done for her litter two years before, frenetically, fastidiously, perfectly. But I wasn't sure of Elsa's help. I was well aware if Elsa was going to be anything like her maternal forebears, her contribution to nurturing the puppies might be limited to lying still while they suckled. And even for that we would be grateful.

Elsa still didn't want to nurse. We would drag her into the whelping box, beg her to lie down. She wouldn't. Then we would have to pull her front legs out from under her and push her rear down. One of us would lie across her, holding her down, while another would put puppies on the nipples. We held her down for the nursing. This was not my Elsa. She was having a terrible confusing time. In those four dozen one hundred count boxes of Earth Bath lanolin-free grooming wipes with a grand total of forty-eight hundred single wipes, I could see the future. I was certain we would use them all. I didn't think we'd ever sleep again.

There are two phrases that strike terror in the hearts of breeders: Fading Puppy Syndrome and Failure to Thrive. The first seventy–two hours are the most dangerous. This is when any real developmental life-threatening failure will show up – digestive systems that don't work, lungs that collapse, brains that bleed. Hawk-eyed and vigilant, I watched for signs—something wrong, something weird, something different. I warned Mamie and Joy to watch them carefully. "If you see anything weird," I told them again and again, "Anything different, alarming, strange, let me know. Whatever it is, the slightest difference, wake me up. And keep counting them. And check the heat." We had two notebooks – one for weights and one for events and directions. I wrote my warnings in with double exclamation points. "And wake me up if you see anything!! And write everything in the book, even stupid things!! Wake me up at any signs of distress!!"

The pups were not gaining yet, but maintaining their birth weights. Their bodies twitched as they slept, growing, swimming across the sea of blankets, sometimes dangerously tunneling under the blankets, or disappearing under Elsa's huge tail, or under the Elsa-sized black and white stuffed toy dog surrogate mother who went into the box when Elsa came out.

I filled the log book with instructions. "Keep counting them!! Don't step in box until you count them. Remove nipples from bottles while heating. Make sure puppies are warm enough. If cold, they pile up. If too warm they spread out far away. They should be near each other. Keep checking the heat. Keep counting!!" Puppies have no heat control. Once they are chilled, it is very tricky to warm them up again. It has to be done slowly and carefully. A blast of cold air can kill them.

There are rules and rules and more rules here in the basement. The first rule is count the puppies every time the mother goes in with them. A groggy mother can roll over them and crush them. Bob had built a shelf in the walls of the whelping box for the puppies to go under and away from their enormous mother but they were too weak to move away those first few days.) Rule two: count the puppies before you go in the box in case one is under the blankets. Rule three: no other dog can come in the room. If another girl or a male comes in the room, the mother might leap up to defend her puppies. I know one breeder who lost two pups this way. Leaping from the box to attack the invading/visiting dog, the mother stepped on two of her pups and broke their tiny necks. Rule four hundred: check the heat constantly. Rule five thousand: report any anomaly, any change, anything that catches the eye -- for example, a puppy lying inert in a corner, away from the other pups. The ultimate rule: wake me up if you have any doubts. Which was the first rule broken.

The Christmas music had given way to the news and I was suddenly wide awake. Joy held Ms. Green toward me. "Something's wrong with her leg and her belly. She's been crying for hours. We didn't want to wake you up."

"Wake me up. Always. For anything. Sleep is not a holy act. We could lose one in the snap of a finger." I was furious but couldn't afford to be. "Good observation, Joy. Good."

I took Ms. Green's temperature immediately, which on a puppy that size demands exquisite aim. I couldn't tell if her distress came from her stomach which was too hard or her leg which she held out straight and dragged behind her as she moved across the blankets. I didn't know if it were orthopedic or systemic or digestive. Or both or all. Systemic could manifest itself in swollen joints and pain. Her temperature was normal therefore probably not systemic. It was orthopedic and/or digestive. She'd hurt herself. How could she hurt herself? What did it mean? What did it imply? Is this failure to thrive? Would I have to put her to sleep? Could the little leg be broken? The bones were so soft, the connections so rubbery. Can a neo-natal have an operation? Why did I have to ratchet every event up to death? "Keep it simple," Bob said to me. "Keep it simple." We gave her a half gram of Bene-bac Gel. She licked her lips. The Bene-bac is basically lactobacillus. It soothes and coats the digestive track. I gave Elsa nine grams. The directions on the back are wonderful: how much for infant tigers, marsupials, bear cubs.

I splashed my face with cold water, asked politely when Elsa had last been out for a potty call. Obviously, she hadn't been. Puppies are more interesting than old lady dogs. I would have to address Elsa's needs with more exclamation points in the notebook. Mamie, Joy, and Elsa went out again into the night. Elsa looked over her shoulder at me to ask if I were coming with them. Elsa was trying to cling to me as Joy was clinging to Mamie.

Christmas carols played endlessly until the news and weather came on briefly. Ms. Green was howling again. I held her against my chest, stuck her in my bra between my breasts, her tiny head under my chin. The puppies were to be fed in the same order each feeding cycle so no one had to wait too terribly long. We would begin the cycle with Mr. Yellow as he was the first one to wake up and complain mightily. I was increasingly worried about the flow of formula from the bottle so the formula had to be strained after we heated it. The bottle nipples were clogging up. We poked holes in them to enlarge them. As soon as I heard Bob walking around above us, I asked him to hit the 24-hour pharmacy for different nipples.

"What kind?" he deservedly asked.

"Get one package of every kind and we'll try them out."

Everything took so much time. The puppies had to be weighed morning and evening. We measured out vitamin drops once a day, gave them Bene-bac Gel for digestion once a day. Ms. Green needed her leg massaged and flexed. I wrote in the logbook: "Flex and extend the left hock and stifle fifteen times three to four times a day. Cover the heat lamps with aluminum foil. And," I wrote stupidly, "Be sure to read the logbook." I wrote a small check mark by Dark Blue's name. He would be Solomon's heir. There was something

72

essentially familiar about him, something elegant in his proportions.

Joy and Mamie came in from the cold, chattering, arguing about Joy's smoking habit. The air changed. Yet again I asked them with exquisite politeness to use another door next time. The air in the room chilled suddenly and filled with the cigarette stench from their clothing. They unwrapped their blankets, shook off the snow. Joy curled up in a bed and was immediately asleep. Mamie, her polar opposite, a machine, decided to organize the kitchen. Snowballs the size of tennis balls hung from the flowing hair on Elsa's legs and sides. I towel- dried Elsa and wrote in the notebook, with many exclamation points, that the puppies could get chilled if Elsa comes in covered in snow. I couldn't relax and I would no longer allow myself a deep sleep and depend on the log book instructions. I had been asking too much of Mamie and Joy. After all, I was the experienced one and these were my puppies. I had to take full responsibility. I could only cat nap. And so I was on watch, alert as I'd never been, present, counting, counting, counting, pulling this one and that one out from a corner, from under a blanket, from under Elsa. The puppies were attracted to Elsa's pungent rear end. Nothing like the smell of afterbirth to attract a crowd. They disappeared under the plume and fume of Elsa's tail as if they wanted to go back where they had come from. Elsa would have to be rinsed off more often, dried carefully. Short-tempered from lack of sleep, I tried to be more informative than critical. It was hard to cover my anxiety. Much later Mamie told me they didn't mind. They were impressed with the way I focused and wondered if I ever wore anything other than a nightgown. I saw no point in getting into street clothes just because the sun had risen. I had a collection of long, over-sized, funny, intersex, flannel night shirts -- leopard skin, cabochon roses, work- shop tools, space ships, ski scenes, snow men, fruits, a few restrained and faded tartan plaids – all of which accessorized beautifully with neon geometric print fleecy socks and turtlenecks of any color.

It wasn't only the puppies who were in danger. Elsa had finished nursing two sets of pups. She climbed out of the box, took a drink of water, and, with a groan, lay down at my feet. She panted heavily until she cooled down. I knew we could trust her not to return to the box by herself. It was the last thing she wanted to do. I went to the bathroom. Joy slept. Mamie mixed and measured formula and Pedialyte in the kitchen. Suddenly we realized Elsa was gone. We called and called, ran to the first floor, the second floor, checked the bedrooms and the closets. She was nowhere. Finally I heard her snoring under the basement steps. Poor sweet thing. She was hiding. This had been a terrible ordeal for her. And she was in pain from her surgery. And those strange creeping creatures were trying to eat her. And she was unbearably warm and exhausted and hungry but unable to eat because she was sick from the anesthesia. I tried to coax her out. Finally, limber Joy climbed under the stairs and pushed her out. Elsa raced away from us through a hallway to her kennel and stood in front of it. I felt terrible for her. She wanted this to be over. All of it -- the pain, the fear, the weakness, those things sucking on her, the heat. Nothing instinctual was happening to Elsa. She had no idea what was going on but was good-natured enough to do whatever we asked of her. Until she could take no more and hid under the stairs. Not until I had my own hysterectomy did I realize how much she must have been hurting. She couldn't take pain pills as they would go into her milk. We had been so focused on the puppies' well-being we had ignored her. I wrote further directions in the logbook. "Elsa's surgery scar has to be cleaned twice daily or more if it smells funky. Please keep her rear end clean. Please pet her often and speak kindly and reassuringly to her." Elsa was still discharging afterbirth liquids. The heat also increased proliferation of bacteria. We had to watch Elsa's wound, keep it clean, keep her bottom clean, watch for maggots under her tail. They look like rice, I explained. Everyone shuddered. Maggots do clean a wound and then they become flies and leave, I assured them. Nevertheless, the very concept, although just a possibility, having never yet happened to us, is completely disgusting. Was it I who had begun life as a princess?

Elsa had to be fed as often as possible, which meant endless arrays of choices for Elsa, most of which were refused. It was absolutely imperative that Elsa eat in order to bring down her milk for those first possible "Failure to Thrive" days. Her milk would protect the pups from disease as it contained immunizing colostrum. The puppies need that protection and could only get it through Elsa's milk. She had to make milk, lots of it. In order to make milk, she had to eat. Enough milk just wasn't coming. The puppies spent a lot of time working the nipples but their bellies were never full and round until we bottle-fed them. I tried to spoon-feed Elsa. She wanted no kibble. We tried bits of liver and corn bread. That worked for three or four bites. She needed her water changed very often. She would refuse stagnant water. In the heat of the room the water turned fast. Without enough water she could dehydrate, go feverish, and dry up whatever milk supply she did have.

While the fox was making daily approaches toward me, Elsa, on the other hand, was distancing herself. "I am not eating. I am not here. Leave me alone." I understood. It was, admittedly, how I dealt with the birth of my own three babies. A natural mother she was not nor was I although my children survived in spite of me. Under duress (which in canine body language transfers to looking backward over her shoulder as if there might be some escape route from the forward predicament) she would climb into the whelping box. Elsa had been forced into the whelping box for three days, twelve times a day. She caught on or gave in. At last, on command, Elsa would lie down, roll over...all on command...allow us to lift one leg to give the puppies better nipple access, and lay still while they suckled. That was the limit of her contribution. She did not clean them, stimulate them, lick, sniff, nibble, interact with them in any way.

Until, at the end the fifth day, Mamie yelled, alarmed, "Look what's she doing! What's happening to Elsa?"

The bellows of Elsa's ribcage and stomach were heaving. We'd struck oil. "Her milk is coming down. She's fine. She's making milk. Lots of it."

"Good girl, Elsa. Good girl. We need your help." She licked my hand. I spoon-fed her Edy's French Vanilla Ice Cream. She licked the spoon, licked her lips, asked for more. Licking of lips has always struck me as a sign from the dogs that they are ready to eat. I fed Elsa a few more liquid spoonfuls. But she was finished. We'd try again and again. One bite for me, one for her. Sometimes it worked.

Joy was wonderful. She spent most of her time in the box, touching the puppies, watching them, cleaning them, talking to them, passing them to me for feeding. She found a bright red belly. "That's scalding," I told her. "It's a burn from urine. Or bleach in the blankets. Is anyone putting bleach in the wash? So wash them off gently. Wash them all off. Luke warm water, no soap. Tell Bob to get some Ivory Snow. No more harsh detergent. And someone's putting bleach in the wash. I smelled it. No bleach!"

Now, as if there wasn't enough to be done, the puppies had to have their bellies washed and dried three to four times a day, their blankets changed more often, and antibiotic cream rubbed on the scalded areas, which were actually staph infections from the acid of their urine. Staph can spread quickly. We had added another endless task.

Ms. Green's leg was not as stiffly resistant. Joy massaged and flexed. The puppy's belly was slightly softer. "Watch for pustules," I wrote into the log book, crossed out pustules, wrote in pimples. How many times did I repeat myself? What did these women think of me haranguing endlessly? "Don't forget the heat. Keep checking the heat. What's that thermometer read? When did you change Elsa's water? Have you guys eaten anything yet? Do you want Bob to go out for pizza? Watch out for the fox when you take Elsa out to pee." It wasn't that I didn't work as much as they did. I just worried more. Joy and Mamie worried about me, constantly reminding me to go to sleep, get the newspaper, make coffee. Which might have meant they were trying to get me off their backs. When the pups were fed, all the tasks done, Mamie would start cleaning and organizing. I asked her where she had learned to clean so well and why so furiously. "My mom beat me and my sister if we didn't clean right. She threw knives at us."

After all the puppies had been bottle- fed and been on Elsa, blankets changed, bottoms and bellies washed, I asked Mamie to pass me Mr. Blue. That was when the identity crises erupted and would engulf us until the puppies left to their new homes. "Which Mr. Blue?" Mamie asked with an edge to her voice. My necklace system had collapsed. "Mr. Light Blue? Mr. Green and Blue, Mr. Turquoise, or Mr. Dark Blue? Or Aqua? Or Aquamarine?" She, too, had lost patience. We had to get more distinct colors of yarn.

I pointed to the one I wanted. Mr. Dark Blue was the one I had first chosen. I could tell from the markings. He looked exactly like his father, Solomon. I lifted him to my face, smelled the puppy breath, put him in my lap, and stroked his velvet back. "Who are you, Mr. Blue? Are you someone I know? Or knew? Were you here before this? As someone else?"

Mamie heard me. "You better go to sleep. You sound like one of my mentals."

The clock ticked loudly above my head. I stood to put Mr. Dark Blue back in the box, tripped into the box, and fell flat. Somehow I was able to suspend Mr. Dark Blue in the air, but I landed on another puppy with my elbow and it didn't move. Joy pulled me upright. I grabbed the washcloth of a puppy, limp, no sound. My heart stopped. I shook the pup. Ms. Pink. Okay, Ms. Pink. I blew in her nose. I rubbed her ribs and belly. Nothing. I did everything we had done when they were first born to clear their airways, swung her, up and down. Nothing. For some utterly counterintuitive reason, I took her out in the bitter cold and shook her there. I don't know why I did this. I suppose I hoped the cold would shock her system. But my litany had been to keep them warm. If she were alive, I was endangering her even further. I cannot imagine what led me to take her outside but it worked. She howled. Thank God. I ran her inside, sat in front of a heater with her, held her to my chest, and kept rubbing her. Mamie put a drop of Rescue Remedy into little Ms. Pink's mouth to stabilize her system. I opened my mouth for a few drops as well. I'd knocked the air out of Ms. Pink but she was fine. How thin the thread. Nothing seemed broken when I moved limbs and touched her head and neck. Joy and I took turns holding her. We gave her an extra feeding of warm formula. She curled up on her blankets and went to sleep, twitching happily away. I felt like one of those comic-strip wimpy men who can suddenly lift a car off an injured child. I didn't know where the idea to take her outside came from but it was something very, very necessary. Ms. Pink was sleeping. The cold air hadn't killed her. I hadn't killed her. It nearly killed me.

There was another heart-stopping moment. Mamie shook me awake for this one. At the far corner of the box Mr. Gray and White was curled up in a ball, motionless. He was breathing but extremely lethargic. I held him as Mamie dropped in some Rescue Remedy. That didn't help. I do this very strange thing with my lethargic African violet plant. The African violet for years had produced one bloom a year -- a sort of erectile dysfunction bloom if that. With sugar water, my African violet crowns herself all winter long, bloom upon

78

bloom upon bloom. She gets sugar in her water. I don't know where I got that idea. But maybe it would work for Mr. Gray and White. I heated water, stirred in sugar, used the dropper to feed it to the baby. I had to force it into his mouth. He was very weak. The syrup dribbled out. But some must have gone in for he stirred and opened his mouth for more. We put him on Elsa's nipple quickly and he suckled, fell off, suckled. We held him on. In a few minutes he was suckling voraciously. Well, for what it's worth, the sugar water extrapolated to Mr. Gray and White. He was alive and well. At the risk of being obvious, I suppose one would agree that necessity is the mother of invention. I just hoped, with each of the emergencies lying in wait among these puppies, we could come up with a save…wherever it came from.

"Wake me up if you need me." And a further Master of the Obvious remark: "And, Mamie, watch Mr. Gray and White." I drifted off and then somehow lights were on. I had slept through a feeding and it was morning. Mamie was yelling at Joy to take her morning meds, to change her clothes, to brush her teeth, to eat something. But Joy was holding Ms. Green, rocking her, talking to her, ignoring Mamie. I finally intervened. Ms. Green's little belly was hard as a rock. Her anus was extended oddly. Which meant constipated. She needed stimulating. Still concerned that the formula was too thick, we added an inch of Pedialyte to the mix. Gold. She pooped. Her belly was softer. Ms. Green still held her rear leg out straight but it was slightly more flexible. She no longer cried out when we touched it. Joy fell in love with this puppy and named her Sephira, name as blessing.

Mamie was quickly taking charge although she was totally obedient to the logbook. I didn't have to rule or confront. I just had to write in the logbook. But if I were to break my own rule, she was quick to point out my crime. I was grateful. I have no ego issues with being told what to do by others. Especially when they ultimately did whatever it was they told me to do anyway. Mamie had not only organized the kitchen but attacked the storage closet. And was busy organizing my husband. "Now you sit down and listen to me," she would carp at him. We were both totally amused. No one gives Bob orders. Somehow, Mamie could. Months after we would have to call Mamie on the phone and ask where things had gone. She was organizing us. I loved it. "Go to sleep now, Rhoda. Bob, bring her a new nightgown. Don't you want to get dressed, Rhoda? And we need more whisks for the formula, Bob. And preemie nipples for the baby bottles. And a dish rack for the bottles. And a smaller bottle brush. These are too big."

Bob slid yet again into his ski jacket, added to his job description that of the supply officer -- which he had been in the Navy when we were just married. In his generous, energetic way, he purchased, each time, six of every item Mamie required even though she had asked for only one. And, because he couldn't find a bottle-drying rack she needed, he constructed one of upright nails on a wooden base which worked perfectly. The things he had to learn since Wharton School!

At last, the Failure to Thrive days were over. The pups were sleeping three hours between feedings. They drank more and more formula every day. They were getting rounder, fuller, more energetic, and forever hungry. They'd all gained ounces, Mr. Yellow more than the others. And Ms. Pink was alive and well. Ms. Green still dragged her leg behind her as she swam over the blankets but her digestive system was on track and we could manipulate the leg quite freely. Mr. Gray and White did not fade again. Mr. Yellow was growing too fast. Elsa agreed to Saltine and Ritz crackers, was on her third carton of Edy's French Vanilla Ice Cream, and had shown some cautionary, albeit temporary, interest in Boar's Head liverwurst and Nathan's Skinless All Beef Kosher Hot Dogs. Her milk was coming down often. Mr.

Yellow acquired a real name: Bulldozer. Bulldozer because he shoved his way sideways across his mother's belly, searching for the particular nipple to which he alone was entitled, knocking his suckling siblings left and right. Bulldozer. I thought perhaps I should keep him as well or instead of Mr. Dark Blue. He weighed more than the others. He had great bone and good markings. Breeders say that at four weeks you can see exactly what the dog will look like full grown, in perfect balance. And not until another two years will you be able to see him in balance again. Choosing a pup from that mass would become an enormous job. Unless somehow the pup chose me. Which happens.

Mamie had to go home. She had been with us night and day for a week. Her daughter was running the group home where Mamie should have been. Now Mamie could only come at night. I had to call two more people who were standing by. So, on the morning of the sixth day I took a shower and put on a sweat suit to impress the newcomers. Mamie wanted Joy to change from pajamas to street clothes. "Come on, come on. I gotta take care of my mentals. I gotta go. What's the matter with you?" After much yelling and threatening, Joy went upstairs and returned in clean sweats. I would find it was a game they played and replayed, relished, every morning, which, I realized meant do you care about me. Finally, certain that Joy was awake and alert and ready to take over, Mamie put on her silver ski jacket, her fur boots (South side garage sale, six bucks), dangled her keys and her very cute hand-painted reading glasses in their hand-painted case (two dollars someplace). She promised that someday she'd take me around to garage sales. I was not happy to have her leave. Nor was she happy to leave. She assured me she'd be back around dinner time, that she lived only twelve minutes away if I needed anything and she'd come in any weather. When I climbed upstairs to the family kitchen (as opposed to our basement dog kitchen), I found that Mamie had brewed coffee, cleaned that kitchen as well, laid out a breakfast sweet roll, napkins, spoons, sugar, coffee cup, juice glass, all lovingly and ladylike. Whoever sent me out into the cold air with Ms. Pink, whoever gave me sugar and water for the African violet and Mr. Gray and White, *that* whoever might also have led me to Mamie.

CHAPTER ELEVEN

At the end of the puppies' first week almost everyone had doubled their weight, even the two little girls although they were still too far behind. Mr. Yellow was moving steadily ahead of the other sixteen. The rest of the puppies, except for Ms. Peach, moved ahead for the first day, slowed down, then moved up. We had to worry about Ms. Peach who didn't gain for three days, but then suddenly she caught on and started gaining. At the end of the first week, most were at or near two pounds and, of course, Mr. Yellow had expanded to two and a half pounds. We recorded weights twice a day, made endless notes, endless directions, and, as in the nature of life, kept changing protocol as the puppies changed. At the end of the second week, except for Ms. Peach (whose owners-to-be had already named her Lucy) all the others were round and substantial. Lucy was struggling to catch up. But she was determined. She nursed hard and strong and fought for her place on a nipple, but she would gain and lose. During some feedings, having worked so hard, she'd fall asleep on the nipple. Then we'd wake her up and offer her formula. Finally, she caught up and actually moved ahead of a few of her sisters. Watching the weights was like watching a horse race, furlong by furlong. Needless to say we watched every ounce and, even though it was Bob's job to weigh them, I often snagged a few clandestine weigh-ins myself. At last, both of our tiny bird-size baby girls were almost as large and certainly as active as their siblings.

If a puppy went off its feed or seemed lethargic, we took their temperatures as well. Once I was in the upstairs family kitchen when Joy, tears running down her face, brought a puppy to me. She also brought the thermometer but had forgotten the Vaseline. It was a long way downstairs to the Vaseline so I chose the short-cut and headed, thermometer in hand, to the dish of soft butter on the counter. Bob caught me. "You're not...you *did* wash it first, *didn't* you?" I assured him I had. "Of course I did. Really!" I had no idea if I had or had not. Probably not. No one seemed any the worse for my short-cut. If taking the temperature of a fully grown dog is difficult, imagine finding the anal equipment of a tiny squirming puppy. Her temp was normal but now her new and utterly buttery intriguing anal scent was beyond the beyond. Her littermates had never smelled anything like it. "Butter! Beyond afterbirth. Life is good!" They enveloped her, assaulted, cleaned, curried, would not leave her intriguing bottom alone until we soaped her up and rinsed her off.

Elsa had become somewhat more cooperative, although hardly eager. I was wary of her emotional stress and hoped she wouldn't break again and try to hide or conceivably...it has happened... attack a puppy. She never went into the whelping box without gentle encouragement but when she was in, she was careful, stepping lightly, lying down, going into her roll over without command and now sweetly lifting her foreleg so the pups would have access to her nipples. We had become a team, Elsa and I. She knew what I needed and she was working with me. And Elsa finally decided to eat, to really eat. With the whether-to-eat issue resolved, we moved into the uncharted crazy-making waters of what-to-eat. I understood completely although my dietary needs were most likely emotionally driven. The last time I had surgery all I wanted was birthday cake (with equal parts of icing, pretty colorful flowers, and white cake) and stuffed cabbage. Elsa settled on Nathan's Skinless Kosher All Beef Hotdogs (although we had purchased much cheaper ones for her), sliced turkey, cornbread, and her ever-ready ongoing supply of Edy's French Vanilla Ice Cream, which she could access at any time and would be replaced often. I remember all my dogs' food preferences. Elsa's mother, Laalaa, during her lying-in, ate only Nabisco Vanilla Wafers and liverwurst. Now and then a Ball Park Hotdog. Elsa's grandmother, Katie, during her lying-in a good ten years earlier, preferred Fruit Loops and cottage cheese. Her C-section was to be at Cornell in Ithaca. A blizzard was coming in. We had to take mother and puppies back to the Best Western Motel for three days where we all had our choice of the complimentary breakfast bar. Katie chose Fruit Loops in cottage cheese which nourished her and, indirectly, her eight newborn puppies until the roads cleared and we could all go happily home.

Normally my dogs eat ordinary kibble with a soup of vegetables and meat. Kibble became a four-letter word now. You can imagine how many varieties of food these post-delivery, post-surgery mothers have to be offered until they settle on something they will eat. And sometimes that choice lasts a few meals and we start again. Liverwurst, shredded cheddar, Honey Bunch Oats, Fage Yogurt, cheap bagged meatballs, Swedish style (less spicy). The list was unending and nutritionally unbalanced. More than unbalanced: dreadful. But, a calorie is a calorie and even more desirable when it contains calcium and protein and loads of fat. Normal healthy dog foods were out of the question. It was no longer a matter of good nutrition; it was a matter of getting enough calories in Elsa so she could produce milk. One prospective puppy buyer (a proud politically Green one at that) dropped out because I wasn't feeding Elsa organic kibble. There was no explaining to that buyer that whatever Elsa agreed to eat, she would get. Kibble, for Elsa, was utterly out of the question, organic or otherwise. Having spent a good portion of her grown life without a stable home, Joy had learned to hide food. She had a stash of junk food under the bed in the guest room. (Various dogs invariably pointed it out to me although they couldn't reach the tantalizing packages) When Joy finally brought her Cheezits down, Elsa nabbed them shamelessly. So Elsa added Cheezits to her diet. Bob brought a dozen boxes from the supermarket. Sometimes Grandma Katie would slip in and polish off Elsa's Cheezits, make short shrift of the ever- present, always-ignored bowl of kibble, and rummage around for the crusts of twelve-grain bread (not wheat, not rye, not white) smeared with peanut butter and wheat germ leavings. One day Katie discovered and, in great, astonished gulps, devoured Elsa's Edy's French Vanilla Ice Cream. What IS this? It's marvelous! Elsa didn't mind that Katie was polishing off her ice cream or her Cheezits. There was always more. Elsa didn't mind if Katie looked at her puppies. Elsa didn't mind anything. She only wanted to be cool. The room was much too warm for her. And she only wanted to sleep. Next to me on the sofa, her back pressed against mine, was her destination.

I suspect, rather than being finicky, there was something the mothers knew which we didn't know. Ten years ago, Elsa's grandmother, Katie, had very little milk, so we gave her pups formula. Back then, some of the commercial puppy formulas lacked amino acids and that lack had been shown to produce cataracts in the pups. So I crushed and powdered amino acid pills and tried to get them into the formula but the chunks invariably were stuck in the nipples of the bottles. I had laid out the amino acid pills I had been crushing on a counter top. I left for a moment. When I came back to the room from the kitchen, the crushed pills were gone. I thought perhaps I'd knocked them off the counter with my elbow. No. Later, I found Katie sniffing at the open pill bottle, poking and pawing at it, clearly trying to knock it over to get at the pills. I have never since seen any of my dogs choose their own pills. Part of me didn't want to believe that Katie was adding amino acids to her milk in her own way. I offered her some by hand and she wolfed them down, bitter and unappealing as they were -- a pill we always had to stuff down her throat in the past cloaked with an olfactory disguise of cream cheese or peanut butter. At any rate, I think it's possible that the pickiness over the food comes not only from the after effects of anesthesia but from a particular dog knowledge of what is needed. Is it possible that Katie understood her pups needed amino acids? You know by now I would assume as much.

By feeding the puppies more often during the day, we ever so slowly expanded their night feedings to longer, miraculous intervals. An extra half hour here, fifteen minutes here. We fed them as soon as they whimpered. They now had razor sharp teeth. They grabbed the bottle with ferocity. Sometimes they missed and nailed our noses. They tore into Elsa's nipples now red with irritation. Their new little needle claws scratched her belly. Elsa showed us that nursing hurt, for now she would sit up to avoid the pups' teeth and toenails. With apology we made her lie down. It is hard to imagine the pain she endured. And yet, she endured it. She was making slight progress as a mother. When it became unbearable, she would stand up and leave a few hanging in the air who, until we caught Elsa, held on for dear life as Elsa ran away.

And, Joy, very carefully, with her young eyes, clipped their tiny translucent toenails. We did the math. Four toenails plus a dew claw on each front leg, four on each back leg. Ten up front plus eight in the rear equals eighteen toenails, times seventeen. Three hundred and six tiny toe nails. And they had to be done every other day to protect Elsa's already painful nipples. Dog toenails which civilians call claws have a line called a quick. If you cut above the quick the nail bleeds. The dog screams. You die of guilt. At which point, fast, you have to cover the bleeding nail with cornstarch and pray the bleeding stops. Lovingly and patiently, Joy sat in the whelping box, puppies climbing over her, nibbling on her toes, exploring, finding ways into her clothes, sleeping in her lap.

87

She sat and trimmed their nails every other day and never once drew blood. Another big A on Joy's report card.

As the toenails grew, so did their coats. They turned from velvety mole- skinned pups to fuzzy pups, not yet fluffy but getting there. Still blind and deaf – their ears flat to their heads, their eyelids pasted down – their sense of place and smell, heat and cold, expanded daily. They had virgin noses and paw pads, still fresh and pink, unfinished... They were to die for. The pups scooted around with increasing energy. Life for the pups centered on Joy. They spent most of the day in the whelping box, and on the surrogate mother toy, and in our laps. They climbed and fell and hid and appeared, tunneled under blankets, grappled with gravity. Any fleshy extension, whether my nose or a brother's privates, was fair game. Their dreadnaught drive was to find a nipple. Where is the nipple? Is this a nipple? It's in the wrong place. Might be. Try. They didn't interact with each other except to push or pass by or over or suck. Their dog toy surrogate mother was as large as Elsa. She was playground and sanctuary. When the count was short and some had disappeared, the first thing we did was shake out the floppy toy. One here, one there, they would suddenly appear from her folds, from between her legs, from her mouth, reborn. They would climb over her, tumble off, climb up again, vanish. One day Mamie arrived with a large purple floppy donkey toy: Eyore of Winnie the Pooh fame, our second surrogate mother. Consciousness expanded rapidly.

We had collected mountains of old blankets from Salvation Army stores around the county. A prospective puppy owner managed housekeeping at a large motel. She arrived one morning with a Jeep filled to the ceiling with faded bedspreads. Had she bleached them herself? The electric blankets with their plastic cords running through them are the best because they are heavier, which means that they lay flat and in place. We also purchased two dozen lovely, soft double-sided fake sheepskin fleecy pads; they turned out to be totally non-absorbent and urine ran right through them. There is an inherent danger in using blankets in the whelping box. Puppies would tunnel under them, get wrapped and trapped, and could suffocate. Or we could step on a living lump and crush it.

When we first began breeding, we lined the box with newspapers. *The Wall Street Journal* has the best absorbency. When we lived in an upscale neighborhood, we would collect stacks of the WSJ from our neighbors. But even the *WSJ* was slick and slippery, hard to stuff in plastic garbage bags – a mess. Now, having gone rural and frugal, we had no available piles of the *Journal*. Other breeders used shredded newspaper. Those piles were also tough to gather up and it was always a worry that the pups would ingest a shred here and there. Blankets were ultimately easier as long as we watched. And counted. And stepped carefully, avoiding both a poopy mess or a puppy hiding under a blanket. I wrote in the logbook too often: "Count before you step in. Count before you step out." If we cut an infinite number of toenails, if we used an infinite number of baby wipes, the times we counted puppies far surpassed those numbers combined. How many thousand times did we count puppies? And recounted because invariably they moved, vanished, or we counted the same one twice or only found sixteen. At which point we gently shook out the stuffed surrogate mothers, and all the blankets until we found him/her happily sleeping away in the warm, dark folds of the blankets, not suffocating, not dead, crushed or broken. As they grew stronger -- muscles and nerves activating-- they could free themselves. We then dared to leave the room, but not for long, nor often. We stopped worrying as much about Elsa rolling over and crushing the pups. She didn't want to go into the box and only climbed in on command.

Up until the first week, the puppies had spent the majority of their time sleeping. They grow while they sleep. I could watch the twitching as nerve and muscle activated. Then they added more and more movement time, exploration time to their agenda. They grew more active every day, hauling their bodies about with their forelegs, traveling. They were not yet strong enough to stand. I sat for hours watching them, dreaming them into adulthood, into the show ring, into the woods, into my bed, into their lives. I'd squint and imagine them full-grown and noble. Ms. Green began to use her back leg some of the time. It was healing. And the scalding was over. Their bellies were clean and healed. Bravely, we set up a baby monitor on the second floor but still, the babies were never left alone.

The puppies needed the warmth and the training of a mother, the touch of love and correction. We cuddled them often but we could not give them what Elsa could and wouldn't. I needed Elsa to be a natural dog. She couldn't. Elsa only wanted to lie next to me or be in the coolness of her kennel run. She would pull herself onto the narrow sofa and press her body into me. I removed the back pillows to make more room and we would sleep tucked into each other, a greater intimacy hath no man. She was not going to be a dog for me, not a mother. Her milk might have arrived but her instincts had not returned. At first I thought Elsa was seeking comfort from me, which of course she was, but then I slowly realized that Elsa, aware of my own tensions, might have been offering me *her* comfort: her great tail over my knees, her warm breath wafting through my hair, a heavy paw on my shoulder. My Elsa. Or maybe she was just making certain I stayed there in the room with her. Or all of the above. To keep her in the room and to soothe her, we brushed her for long periods, kneaded her spine, rubbed her forehead and eyes, worked what animal caretakers know as the Tellington Touch on her body, over and over again, in circles, little clocks of love. And tried to feed her.

One night we watched the puppies creep under the shelves and then form a little parade within the walls of the whelping box. Everyone moved from left to right under the shelves around the box, again and again, a strange and steady, secretive movement. They hugged the inside wall, moving in line like ants, pulling themselves along with their front legs, moving in a purposeful path within the perimeter of the whelping box, going in the same direction, on a mission. This continued for days, always under the shelving, always from left to right. I know that grown dogs are cautious about stairs, particularly when one side of the stairwell is open. They hug the wall as they climb. And of course dogs love to be under something or in something whether a crate, a shelf, a desk, or the dining room table. So the puppies, perhaps, were afraid, and hugged the wall and remained under the shelf as they explored their world with a purpose we would never understand. Perhaps they were practicing FORWARD. Perhaps they were learning UP and DOWN, UNDER, and OVER and OOPS from their dog and donkey surrogate mothers. Now and then, one or the other, would lift up on all fours, wobble, fall down, scramble, up again, forward, wobble, totter, stumble, tumble: funny, little drunken sailors. We laughed at them. We shouldn't have. This was very serious work they were doing. They were working so hard at being dogs. Their front structures expanded; their bodies grew rounder. They were beginning to look more like puppies than moles.

When I had a few moments to sleep, I couldn't sleep. My mind was racing. Even though everything was in order, all the directions clear and concise, there is always that fluidity, the sudden change, the sudden onset. Elsa's pups were moving, almost up and about. They had already gone from slithering to creeping to standing to wobbling on all fours and even moving forward. Soon they would need higher

91

enclosures. Soon they'd outgrow their whelping box, be able to stretch enough to climb up on the shelves of the whelping box and walk around on them. Heart stopping, their little aerial acts. Even though we removed the shelves, in a few days the pups would be able to stretch up to the top of the box's wall, and, within a few more days, stretch and stretch, pull themselves up, and finally tumble out to explore the universe. They all needed heavier confinement and more space. Did I remember to tell everyone to slip the boards into the slots of the whelping box door so Elsa's pups couldn't escape? Had I told the puppy caretakers that puppies can get dehydrated quickly and that the way to tell is to pinch the skin at the back of their neck or by examining inside their lips? Did I tell them if the skin tents up or the inner lip is sticky, they're dehydrated which is life-threatening and they must report this to us no matter what time it is? Did I tell everyone everything they needed to know? Is Elsa off-lead when she goes outside? Did I warn everyone not to let her run, to put her on leash, to watch out for the foxes as she might chase them, rip out her stitches, run away? Someone better wash the dog and donkey mother toys. I had to sleep. I said my prayers. Beginning first with the thank you parts, I relaxed. But as soon as I arrived at the pleases, I was wide awake. That's one way to stay up all night: rehearse all the things that worry you and then try to go to sleep. Prayers didn't work. Or maybe they do work. They just didn't put me to sleep.

Elsa's stitches were ready to come out. My hands were too shaky to snip at them. The skin around them was red. A friendly vet tech we'd known for years stopped on her way home and cut the stitches as I held the ballooning breasts away from the wound. When she was through she examined the pups and Elsa carefully and then called Kerry's office to report in. All was well. The next day we bathed Elsa, put her under the blow dryer, brushed her, trimmed long hairs from her rear end that were getting caught up in the afterbirth she was still dripping. I'd been through motherhood three times.

I remember the pain. Removing the stitches didn't help. When Elsa lay at my feet, she curled into a ball. If she were comfortable she would have stretched out.

When I was alone in the room with the puppies I could allow daydreaming – what Mamie referred to as my being "mental", a state I no longer shared publicly. I could talk to the puppies, make promises, give advice, pray for them. Crazy as it may seem, each time I knelt over the whelping box I felt I was looking at immortality, at a continuation of soul, a kaleidoscope rearrangement of familiar molecules – some activated, some silenced. And there they were before me, the little souls of other bodies, now materializing on the fleecy blankets, much the same way Elsa and Mamie had materialized out of the dark, entered the field of barn lights, and stood whole at the back door, from idea to shadow to shape.

Six years ago Mary Long, our animal communicator, had told me that when Bumper was born, her grandmother Ishtar (dead a few years) came in like a tornado, and took her over. In her early months, puppy Bumper limped. And she said to Mary Long that she didn't know if she herself was hurting or if she was feeling someone else's pain. For me, that was an acknowledgment that another dog soul was present, a dog who had known pain. Eventually Bumper stopped limping. Others might call her limping a case of puppy growing pains. Vets would call it panosteitis which means wandering lameness. "Mentals" such as myself might call it Old- Soul-In-New Body-itis. Had Great grandmother Ishtar become a part of the puppy Bumper? I don't know. I'd like to think so as I have desperately missed Ishtar. There are so many stories of newly arrived dogs (whether puppies or grown) who come into homes where old dogs have died, who take up their corners, their beds, their toys, their behaviors: old souls arriving, entering into new bodies. When one of my dogs dies I know, somehow (emphasis on the indefinable somehow, which may simply be hope) they'll be back in some shape, some consciousness, if only a lonely persistent all too familiar bark from the woods or a faint movement of an almost-real etheric tail swishing near my knees. Macy, a Newf who died at fifteen, had a little organ that played the Nutcracker Suite. When she died (on the very day Lakota Indian healers had predicted) not only did all the clocks in the house stop, but the Nutcracker Suite organ turned itself on. Nemo, the father of my Solomon, seemed to have also been able to direct energies and send messages as well: when Nemo died a radio in a spare bedroom turned on and played the one song the owner's father always sang to her as a child: Kay Kyser singing, in 1936, *Three Little Fishies*. Anyone out there remember the three little fishes in the itty bitty pool who swam and swam right over the dam? Was there meaning here? An intention from beyond? A message? A goodbye? A hello? Somehow, Nemo, or perhaps the owner's dead father, or coincidence had turned that song on by itself at the very moment when a message had to be sent. Sheer coincidence is an explanation I have learned to doubt. I began to pay attention to the impossible, the synchronicity, the signs.

Years after my first dog Ben died, when I was recuperating from a shattered ankle, I woke up to see him, clear as day, his huge paws over the arm of a turquoise leather chair. The vision, hallucination, sensation was so very real to me I worried about his claws scratching the leather arm. Another time, I saw Ishtar, lifting off the floor just as I woke up in a hospital recovery room. I've heard her bark many nights: a singular evenly spaced bark, which always had been my name.

So there I was on my knees at the whelping box paying attention. I lifted Mr. Dark Blue to my face; he nuzzled, explored, sniffed, then bit my nose which perhaps resembled (possibly maybe- could-it-be?) a very large and available nipple. His world was filled with possibility and possibility was always in the form of a nipple. "Mr. Dark Blue, I think we're going to keep you. You are very special.

94

Who are you, Mr. Dark Blue? Who are you? Who will you be? Who were you? Do you have any messages?" My kindergarten vision was of a crowd of angelic dogs hovering over these puppies, fighting over which one they wanted to become, jostling with each other, shoulder to shoulder, choosing one to enter, shopping for a new vehicle for THE BIG ONGOING JOURNEY. "This time I get the four-wheel drive and the moon roof." "I want to be the one with the three black spots on her back." "I want to be the one with the white stripe on his nose." I believe, or maybe someone taught me, or maybe I read it in something I'd written, that behavior is genetic, which is, for me, a materialistic, scientific way of saying the soul continues. I recognize dogs long gone, barely related, in puppies. I recognize their personalities -- not just similar actions or physical resemblances, but clusters of reactions, of interactions, of attitudes, activities, of play moves, methods of greeting. Bob and I would always seek the dead dog in the new living one. "This one lies still when you approach and flaps his tail on the ground, just once, like a beaver, just the way Joey did. And he only wants to play with Joey's old torn and faded big clutch ball. Being with him is like being with Joey. Isn't it?" we'd ask and assure each other. "And isn't Katie just as pushy and smart as her grandmother, the legendary Ishtar?" Sometimes it's hard to put a finger on their actions which suggest inherited personalities. Sometimes you just feel it. "And that one has to take a shoe outside with him just like the first Ben did. Do you think he's Ben?" Bob and I smile at each other. We don't really believe in the returns but we sure would like to. Or do we? Or do we dare? Sometimes I think that if our totally unrealistic beliefs – our form of dog worship -- was organized into a collective religion, we'd all be on our knees. I was, both literally and figuratively, on my knees.

95

We've spent so much energy on Elsa, her moods and her menus, it isn't fair to leave their father Solomon out of our story. In some litters, the female makes the more obvious imprint on the puppies. In this litter Solomon, at least in terms of the markings, made the greater imprint, and, I suspect markings are an indication, a surface clue of a cluster, of deeper imprints: size, personality, health, structure. Solomon was two years old when he fathered all these puppies. I watched Solomon in the ring at the Westminster Kennel Club show at Madison Square Garden. When he entered the ring, head-high, powerful, beautiful, tears ran down my face. When he was a three week old puppy he stared at me. He never took his eyes from me when I was in the room. His littermates had very short-lived interest in me unless I was bearing food. His staring at me was something entirely deliberate, stunning. He had chosen me. When Mary Long "interviewed" Solomon, she said, "He is 'celestial'. He sees everything. Like a star. His destiny is to go out to the world. Solomon is already out there. He says that there's a whole planet to love here. He is like Ishtar. He can look down and see everything in perfect selflessness. Our world is filled with miniature star beings," she went on. "There are other worlds trying to reach you." One had, I'm sure, reached me.   In my perverse way of receiving information, I had already given him his American Kennel Club registration name: Stargazer. I chose that name to mean he was looking at the stars because King Solomon of ancient times had studied the stars. I was wrong. The name I chose meant, Mary Long told me, that this dog Solomon was looking down *from* the stars. As if, as if, he were a star being. "Beings from other worlds," Mary Long, explained, "beings who are trying to reach you. Solomon reached us." And somewhere in the thriving writhing pile of the Elsa and Solomon litter of puppies, there were more Solomons who had "gotten through". "Is that what you were?" I asked Mr. Dark Blue, "A star being?"

One morning I was measuring out the day's worth of formula (dry powdered puppy formula, Pedialyte, boiled spring water, Karo syrup) in the basement kitchen when I heard a blood-curdling puppy scream. Mamie, who had been upstairs having a cup of tea, raced downstairs. She'd heard the scream on the baby monitor. I was certain the fox had somehow found his/her way in. No. Ms. Orange was screaming. She stood in a corner of the whelping box, under a shelf, and she was stuck in puppy traffic. It wasn't pain or terror we heard. It was road-rage. Someone in front of her wasn't moving out of the corner and she couldn't continue what seemed to be a most necessary perambulation, nor did she have either the patience or the intelligence to move around the deaf and obdurate pup. We lifted the pup out of Ms. Orange's way and off she went on her drunken haul. Mamie and I looked at each other. "Sell this puppy." Mamie advised, quite wisely. "She's going to need a lot of attention. What a temper!"

I wondered if Ms. Orange was the same one who complained so bitterly the moment she was born when we were rubbing them to consciousness, when the vet tech called her a bitch, offending me deeply. Ms. Orange would go to a home where she would get lots of attention and lots of training. Driven as she was, she would probably be a fine and competitive athlete. I made a note in the log book as to her strong character. She could go to a show home because of her confidence and attitude. There are particular tests to determine personality which are given at day forty-nine. Watching them 24/7 gives us far more insight. Ms. Orange's noise fell, as they say, on deaf ears. The puppies couldn't yet hear anything, not even her piercing scream. And after a few days, having recognized her scream, we ignored her road-rages as well. She was a female Bulldozer. Bulldozer, however, didn't have a temper. He didn't need a temper or a sound. He just bull-dozed.

Days passed, eased. The more energy the puppies spent, the more they ate. The more they ate, the longer they slept. The longer they slept, the longer we slept. One morning Mamie came running to me with a puppy in her hands. "The ears. Look! See? They're coming." There was a thin slice of light between their ears and their cheeks. Were their ears finally developed? Were they ready to hear? We turned the soft Christmas music off and found a station with loud and strident march music. Classic Russian something. I don't know what it was. The nanosecond I turned that music on, the entire group froze, galvanized, located the sound, snapped around to its source. As one. Left *face*! They could hear. One barked, a small bark, but a bark nonetheless, a dog bark. Where did that come from? "Okay, guys, which one of you barked?" They were almost dogs.

We couldn't wait for the next step: eyes. Day 12 was our goal for eyes. Every morning I'd hold a few up to the window light and look for the glint. And sure enough, at last, there was a glint where the eyes should be. Just a glint. But we were ecstatic. Joy made big notes in the log book. It was she putting in the exclamation points this time. I had to control myself: do not push the lids open. Do not push the lids open, Rhoda. The next day Ms. Red and Green (Ms. Christmas) was the first to have both eyes open. I drew her into my face and she threw her head backward, away from me. Had she seen my white blob of a face or perhaps smelled my weird and disgusting human breath? One by one during the next few days we saw the glint and then the eyes and, even though they could barely see anything, it was wonderful because we just made believe or assumed or hoped they were looking at us. Finally one of them thrust her head toward mine as if she really wanted to see what I was, as in, get-a-closer-look–this–

might-be-important. It was. It was me. She was looking at me! "Oh, it's you. They told me about you, about people. Hello, there." Talk about being present. That look, that curiosity, that acknowledgement of me by this gift of the universe, the wonder of it, the magical validation, was one of those utterly I am present moments for me. The puppies gave me a new identity, enlarged me somehow, connected me to something larger, much larger than myself. Back to the lattice work under my grandmother's porch and the feral cats.

Bob and Mamie were in charge of the laundry or, more accurately, the laundry was in charge of Bob and Mamie. They couldn't keep up. I would wake up from one of the sofa beds and find them sitting together on the other sofa bed, folding blankets and towels, talking softly at midnight, two or three or four a.m. Their rules to live by were so similar: you finish your work and then you rest. In my family, the motto was "the dishes will look better in the morning." The Bob and Mamie One-Day All-Night Laundry Service consumed more time than my jobs. Elsa was still discharging the bloody globs and fluids of afterbirth and the pups were not quite evacuating at will but losing their waste here there and everywhere, all of which increased the laundry load exponentially. Every day there were more loads of laundry than the day before. The piles grew higher. We'd run out of blankets and towels. Sometimes my only choice was to turn the dirty blankets over to their cleaner (maybe) sides and wait for the washed blankets to dry. Now and then I'd grab blankets from the dryer and lay them out, hoping the heat lamps would dry them. The dryers worked without pause. A few times, poor Bob had to load the fuming collection and go to the local Laundromat where, he reported, he was no longer particularly welcome.

Finally the puppies agreed on a corner under a shelf of the whelping box as bathroom. It was a welcomed development. Bladder and bowel control had kicked in. Within no time, that corner had a lot of traffic. The passing pups often left their new bathroom with more poop on them than they had left behind. Which added a new on-going task: more bathing. We filled a square baking pan with baby shampoo and lukewarm water, bathed them. If we were lucky, we could just wipe a crusty spot off with the four thousandth baby wipe. We rubbed the clean pups dry under the heat lamps. Bathing them was my favorite task. I loved to rub their fur the wrong way, lifting the nap to see if their fur was growing. It was, little by little. Their tiny bodies would twitch under my fingers.

The days were intolerably long, the nights even longer, but soon, we would move forward and leave those precious moments behind. Too soon. Not soon enough.

CHAPTER TWELVE

The news was out; a record-breaking Newfoundland litter had arrived in New York State. It was out on You Tube, it was out on the Newf Chat Line, a site for owners. A video of the seventeen newborns in the incubator circulated. We had calls from everywhere: Russia, Mexico, Japan. People wanted to buy puppies, many in pairs. We had far more buyers than puppies. It was much too early for me to even think about selling these pups. Now Bob added something to his job description: answering the phone. Not only did he have to keep track of the twice-daily weigh-ins, the morning drops of antibiotics and vitamins for the pups, the unending laundry, the daily and twice-daily grocery store and drug store runs, but he had to respond to the phone calls. Everyone wanted puppies. Bob wanted to help people find the perfect puppy. And we only wanted to find the perfect homes. When people want a puppy, we insist they come to the house no matter where they live. And when they come they are greeted by five or six Newfies at the door. It's the test. They better not back up, wipe off the slime, flinch, or it's over. There would be a lot of visitors after the pups had their vaccinations, but none now except the Hamlins who came to help.

Four of the Hamlin Most Valuable Player family arrived nightly for the feedings, often bringing dinner: Dave, his wife, Vicky, daughter Kathy, and her fiancé Greg. Sometimes I'd take a dinner out of the Omaha Steak offerings, stick it in the microwave, and just point in the direction of the lasagnas, stroganoffs, or the endless chicken-rice- mushroom soup casseroles I'd prepared weeks before for Elsa (no, thank you) and for us. The Hamlins would change into scrubs or clean clothing they'd left with us, fresh slipper socks, wash their hands, and get to work. Six or seven of us would sit on the two sofa beds. Most often Joy-- because she was far more supple than the rest of us -- would kneel in the box and pass out puppies. Mamie marched around, gimlet-eyed, a drill sergeant. I deferred to her; it was much easier. A puppy sputtered and lost its milk. Mamie would snap: "Not too fast. Get another nipple for that bottle. The milk's running too fast from that one. Hold her up straighter." "That one you just put back is complaining. Put him up on your shoulder and burp him. Yes, just like a baby. Harder. That's it." And then the puppy would offer a deep and impressive burp, larger somehow than itself, and we would all cheer. I would move around and feel bellies to see if they were not full, full, or too full. I'd burp them a second time before they went back into the whelping box. Bob bent over the scale and wrote in their weights. We had an on-going argument about the weighing-ins. I wanted to weigh them after they ate because the fatter they were, the happier I was. He thought it far more logical to weigh them before they ate. So he weighed them before they ate and, after he left the room…well, you know.

When the puppies finished on their bottles and on Elsa, we would all rub their little privates, hang the puppies over waste baskets, and try to catch the outcomes of our stimulation. It was what Elsa was supposed to do. She didn't. There were never enough wastebaskets. We played waste basket soccer, kicking the plastic-lined baskets back and forth to each other, announcing our successes (as if we were responsible for bowel movements) and our failures which were most often announced with an "Oh, Shit." And everyone laughed at the double entendre. "There's some on your lap." "Basket. Quick. I need the basket. Too late." Never had urine or poop been so very interesting and so amusing. Why we limited ourselves to two baskets among seven people I'll never know. Perhaps because it was funny. We celebrated those lives, those miracles. The lonely and frightening hours were dispelled by bad jokes and good friends, really good friends. We never thought to order more waste baskets for our soccer game. I, in fact, thought about taking one of them away and upping the ante of our evening feedings. Elsa was interested in what we were doing, taking one puppy at a time, stimulating, produced urine and poop. She walked among us, sniffing, pawing at us to be petted, but in no way assisting. She only wanted to visit.

One of the most special visitors the puppies had was their big old Great Great Granddaddy, Packard – a large powerful black elder with a generous heart and sweet humility. For days he had begged to come into the whelping room. Most mature male dogs want nothing to do with puppies. I've heard they might kill them. I've seen the males race away, backwards, thinking the pups might be prey, unsure of what to do, confused and fearful. But not Packard. At last, one day when Elsa was being walked we let Packard into the room. He sniffed around, polished off another pile of Cheezits, flattened himself next to the opening of the whelping box, and laid his great nose inside the box. His nose was the size of two puppies. He barely breathed he was so still, watching, sniffing, watching, enraptured. Was he remembering his infancy? Was he learning? Did he want to play? To help? To watch over them? I knew he was trying to look small.

It's charming to see these huge animals when they are trying to assure other creatures that they won't hurt them. Does an animal have self-awareness? Philosophers and behaviorists pose this question often to show that animals have no souls, no conscience. Of course they have. Packard knew he was Packard, knew he was big, and he knew he had to be small. He knew who he was, his size, his shape. Dogs will go flat in front of a small child. "See, I'm as small as you. I can't hurt you." I once saw Theo, Elsa's huge father, trying to convince a frog to play with him, actually making play bows to the frog. A play bow is an amazing invitation/promise of the dog world. All dogs understand it. They all agree upon it. It is a rare and neurologically challenged dog who will break the promise and go for blood. The play bow is a clear never-broken commitment to play without hurting. The rear end goes up in the air; the front end down on the ground with the front paws stretched out. Often the dogs will pause in their wild play and perform another play bow, reassuring each other that this fighting is still all in fun. The frog, however, remained quite stubbornly unconvinced by Theo's play bow, which Theo continued to repeat in the hopes the frog would play. The frog did hop about in a frenzy of fear, which, I believe, Theo happily continued to interpret as an invitation to play. "Don't worry," his play bow said again and again. "I'll be small. I won't hurt you. Promise." The frog finally expelled something dreadful from his mouth which left Theo coughing and salivating until we flushed most of the poison out with a syringe.

I liked Packard very much. He was a gentle and kind, steady animal, very much like Solomon. His calm presence in the puppy room didn't alarm Elsa at all. When she returned from outside, she took no notice of him with his big nose inside the whelping box, but simply stepped over him and up onto the sofa where I wiped the snow from her legs. As far as Elsa was concerned, Packard was not there, puppies were not there, and she, as much as possible, was not there.

If there was one major quick-sand problem with this huge litter, it was keeping their identities straight. As I write this, I can't even reconstruct the mess that it was. I still can't figure it out. What I do know is that we started out with ten boys and seven girls, assumed for weeks that was what we had, but ended up with eleven boys and six girls. Don't ask. And it all had to do with the necklaces. Within a few days the yarn of the necklaces would stretch so much from the puppies creeping about we would have to crochet a new set, and another slightly larger set, and then another and another and another for weeks until we could purchase real dog small collars for them. All had necklaces of different colors. But the necklaces just weren't working. Not only did the necklaces stretch and fall off but whites turned to grays, yellows to grays, pinks to grays, and the brilliant triple pink, white, gray necklace fused nicely into a singular gluey dirty beige. Necklaces would turn up in the laundry, disappear entirely, change color, fade, absorb a darker color in the wash or, against my wishes, Mamie would pour bleach in the laundry. That's what they did in Mamie's Developmental Center: bleach in the laundry and in the glasses and in the dishes. She'd forget even after I reminded her because it was such a habit of hers.

Bleach was also not a good thing for the puppies' bellies or digestive systems and may have contributed to the initial scalding on their bellies. Whatever didn't already work with our necklace identities was exacerbated by the bleach. Our worst necklace problem continued to be distinguishing among the blues and greens. Turquoise was called Blue/Green, sometimes Light Green, which was often short-handed to Green, sometimes Aqua, depending who was making notes in the logbook and who had donated the yarn. You get the picture – murky to say the least. I think that's where our problem began. We would run out of yarn. Then new yarns arrived and were vaguely different than the originals. Colors shifted, were labeled differently by the note-takers. Maroon became purple. Purple became lavender. Lavender became orchid. When the red lights of the heat lamps shone on the puppies, everything became red. I vowed that someday I'd find a better way to identify them. Some breeders actually shave various parts as in right leg, left leg, rear, to distinguish the pups from each other. Mine didn't have enough hair to count. I thought perhaps nail polish on their heads. Some breeders do use a stripe of paint. Are there seventeen shades of nail polish? Are there seventeen shades of Magic Marker? Eventually we would be able to buy puppy collars in the pet store. But how would we find seventeen pet store dog collars in seventeen different colors? What about pony-tail scrunchies? Bob brought multiple packages of them from the drugstore. There were enough colors. The puppies looked like little dinosaurs with great circular bony shields behind their heads—triceratops -- missing only the three facial horns of that vanished species. Little legs were caught up in their scrunchies. We would find a puppy hobbling about, a foreleg up around his neck. Some, having nailed another's scrunchy, would then trap and drag a screaming sibling across the whelping box. Soon the scrunchies were too tight. So much for scrunchies. Back to yarn. We'd be crocheting for six weeks or more. Mamie was losing patience. Note-taking and weights had become a morass. I had given up.

We tried to identify the pups by their markings. Some of the pups were basically black. Some were mostly black with white – a little more white on one side of her neck, a long black tail with a little white tip. Some were mostly white with black. Some had spots. A few had white stripes on their noses. And they kept moving, vanishing, appearing. Just as annoyed as I was, Mamie held up two pups and two necklaces. "I don't know which ones these are." Fortunately we could check their weights from the night before in the log book. Mr. Green had weighed an ounce more than Mr. Turquoise. There wasn't much difference between the colors which only added to the confusion. There wasn't much difference between the markings of the two pups. We weighed them again (they had both gained some ounces) and dressed them in the appropriate new necklaces. Or had we? We weren't sure we had it right but their weights were so similar…well, who would ever know? "Don't tell Bob," I advised. "It will make him crazy." Not being gifted with logic,

I thought it was amusing when logic didn't work. In this maddeningly fluid situation, the logical grid, the careful spreadsheets, the weight charts we filled out every day had limited use. In fact, became useless. You could feel a puppy's ribs if he were too thin or too fat. The puppy was the territory. The charts were only maps and maps in hindsight at that. Shortly after the mix-up, we realized, upon careful examination, that Ms. Green was actually our Mr. Green. Nope, we had two Mr. Greens. Not ten boys and seven girls. Eleven boys and six girls. Well, the map just isn't the territory. We could have identified them by simply turning them over and looking at their little pink private parts which remained pink no matter how often they were washed. All the records had to be changed. We had to tell Bob as he was keeping the records on the computer in orderly, precise fashion. Our grid on the information was a little less precise, to say the least. Bob didn't think it was funny. I did only because it was all so ridiculous. There was nothing else to think. My mind simply swarmed with confusion. Whatever the confusion was, one thing was certain: there were no puppies dragging a bad leg across the whelping box. Whoever had been Ms. Green was all better. Long after Elsa's litter another breeder told me, "Cat collars. They have many sizes and hundreds of different designs." Next time.

We added two more puppy sitters -- a friend of Mamie's (who also didn't sleep nights) and a very smart totally inexperienced very cool New Age journalist who needed cash for her heating bills and lived up the road. This was clearly not going to be a profitable project. There was already too much money going out in supplies and salaries.

CHAPTER THIRTEEN

Using clamps, Bob had attached (sort of) a rickety metal exercise pen to the open door of Elsa's whelping box, doubling the size of the space. The pups could now move from their wooden enclosure to their fenced enclosure, in and out, in and out. Stronger and larger, they were eating more, eliminating more: a city of pups with no sewage system. Five or six could easily knock down the exercise pen extension which they often did. Every moment, it seemed, they increased their mobility, their brain size, and the resultant curiosity. Now they were climbing, clambering, scooting, and stretching to see over the barrier separating them from Elsa's milk, for their turn at the nipples. They had not been able to see through the wooden sides of their whelping box, but now they could watch everything through the wire work of their x-pen. They lined up, shoving to get out, to see, to be, to go go go. They often sprang the clamps, knocked the pen down, and were soon out sliding, swimming around the linoleum floor. I loved their energy and their curiosity and their determination. But they would splay out on the floor and I was afraid they would damage their hips.

Elsa, of course, hated being there. She didn't want to stay in the puppy room even outside of the whelping boxes. She was content only if I stayed in the room with her. Puppies need the interaction with their mother; aside from the nursing, they need the corrections, the warmth, the presence. Elsa fought to leave the box as soon as the pups were off her nipples. But no. If she could, she'd make a wild dash upstairs to my bedroom, to the center of my bed and bury herself in the comforters. I don't know if she was still hiding, running away, or simply seeking comfort and me. Now that she was dripping afterbirth sharing our beds was unthinkable. Someone would find her, put her on leash, drag her to the pups, lay her down in the x-pen area, drop a board to block half the puppies inside the whelping box (A Team), and place the other voracious half (B Team) on her nipples. The puppies left behind, smelling their mother and dinner, clustered frantically at the wrong side of the board, screaming and scratching to get to the source of all things. I'm sure their screams added to Elsa's distress. Elsa would try to leave, knock down the x-pen. Puppies would follow her, some still attached, hanging onto the nipples like a Calder mobile. We'd collect the errant pups, pop them off the nipples, drag Elsa back, and ask her to lie down again. She would. I had the feeling she was trying, trying very hard, but couldn't stand it. When the eight or nine pups (the B Team) were nursing, we would grab the A Team pups and bottle-feed them. And when the B Team on Elsa fell off the nipples, exhausted or full, they were moved into a portable kennel replete with heat lamps. Then the bottle-fed A Team was attached to Elsa's buffet and the second seating began. While A Team nursed and B Team was still in the portable kennel, we were able to pick up, shake out, wipe up, change blankets, wipe up the coating of mustardy poop that seemed to cover everything. The whelping box refurbished, the screaming B Team puppies would go back into the clean whelping box and we'd pick them up to bottle- feed them, then bathe them. I had no choice. I hired two more women, one for the days, one for the nights. We were all very tired.

Even though there were two stuffed surrogate mamas in the whelping box, it was Joy who was the true surrogate mama. She stayed in the box with the pups for hours, cuddling, patting, moving and assuring them. They would find their way up her pants legs, under her shirt, into her lap, bite fingers, ears, and toes. Joy was totally dedicated. Especially so since Elsa's pups always needed a bath. Their bellies and legs were mustard- colored with poop. Because the population was so dense, the pups would climb through, step into, roll into, and lie in a deposit. Now and then I'd notice a Gold Star pup stop at a mess, sniff, and repulsed, take a turn away; they were learning – a sign that things would get better. We were on constant watch to pick up the soft poops, turn blankets over, cover up a mess with a towel until we could move everyone again. One of our endless activities was washing our socks.

Our main responsibility was to remember which puppy had been fed. The more tired we were, the more quickly memory failed. The finale of the feeding ritual was feeling all the bellies for fullness in case we missed anyone. The logistics were demanding. I was continually asking who's where and what have we done and what's next. When Elsa's painful nursing ordeal was over, she hot-footed it back to the cool safety of her own indoor-outdoor run, turned her back on us, shoved her blankets aside, and collapsed on the chill of her concrete floor. Elsa's nipples and the aureole surrounding them were red with scratches and hot with inflammation. I couldn't treat her nipples other than a pat with cool water. Finally I broke the rules, broke open a Vitamin E gel and squeezed the gel on her nipples. I hoped the vitamin wouldn't compromise the puppies' digestive system. It didn't. I allowed Elsa one Vitamin E treatment a day. Her nipples bled. Another week, Elsa, dear, dear Elsa. They'll be on cereal in another week. It will be over soon, I promise. We were all trying so hard. I mostly to stay awake and keep track of what was happening. I had a lot of trouble keeping track of the A team, B team rigmaroles.

Susan, a skilled technical writer who lived nearby and knew nothing about puppies came aboard. Joyce Red Hat because she belonged to the Red Hat Society and purchased red things as a hobby, came at midnight, Susan, at sunrise. We rejoiced at the welcome roar of journalist Susan's old red rust bucket Jeep. Joyce would pack up and leave; Susan would take over. Not that Mamie, Joy, Bob or I could stop. Mornings were the most demanding of times. Among her endless always fluctuating job description (did you remember to look for fox prints in the snow?), it was now Susan's job to give all the puppies vitamins every morning. And Bob would stumble down stairs to weigh them because the vitamin dose had to be calibrated to the weight changes every day. I was probably undoing the accurate measuring of the vitamin dose with the vitamin E on Elsa's nipples. I just couldn't sacrifice Elsa so completely.

Organizing the world is not my high card. I wanted everyone to love me and love my puppies. It was hard to criticize, hard to be the boss. Now and then, under pressure, Mamie yelled at me and, unbelievably, at Bob who could be a curmudgeon. It didn't matter as long as the work was done. When she was angry or tired or sick (aside from the trauma of those thirty one knee operations, she had fibromyalgia) she would activate into a work frenzy, mop floors, rearrange cabinets, wash more laundry, bathe a dog, rinse Elsa's bottom of its bloody leakings, take over. More and more I turned to Mamie and Susan to run the schedule.

CHAPTER FOURTEEN

Elsa was too human, Celeste far more instinctual, wilder. Perhaps that's why Celeste was such a success as a mother and Elsa such a failure. Or perhaps the differences between Elsa and Celeste were evolutionary. Perhaps Elsa was on her way to a deeper domestication and just couldn't be an instinctive dog any longer. Her "dogness" had been overwhelmed by our ways of life. Celeste had every dog instinct. She was all dog, with a strong trace of the wild, an adventurer. She liked nothing better than surprise attacks from a high point onto an unsuspecting relative wandering below the hill. Not that she hurt anyone except once when her own daughter surprised her and triggered a terrifying unpredictably aggressive reaction. I could predict Elsa's behavior. I didn't know enough to predict Celeste's.

Now that Elsa was a mother, she exhibited no instincts whatsoever. She ran away from her pups and hid. She was too human or at least too humanized, certainly overwhelmed. I would discover it was more than a lack of instinct. We all felt so badly for Elsa, wished she could enjoy her puppies. But she couldn't.

While Elsa was physically recovering well, psychically she was a disaster. When Celeste had her litter, she'd been as natural a mother as one could wish. Elsa's fear was so unnatural, I wondered if it might have been that Elsa recognized and reflected my own tension. Trainers say that emotions go right down the leash from human to dog. I'll bet they go up the leash as well. Elsa might have been saying it was too much for her because she knew it was too much for me. It might have been that Elsa mirrored my anxieties, my tensions. It was difficult not to compare Elsa's lack of mothering to what we had experienced with Celeste when she had her litter. With her first litter, Celeste allowed her pups to nurse well into their ninth week, three or four weeks longer than usual. On the other hand, Elsa found nursing unbearable.

Our days with Celeste's litter had been triumphs. With only ten puppies, which now seemed a small amount, our time with her was calm. She did most of the work, was entirely trustworthy as a mother but we dared not let any other dogs near her whelping box. Unlike Elsa, Celeste wanted to stay in the whelping box with her pups. Two days out of surgery, Celeste, true to herself, acted as if nothing had happened to her. The puppies were the best new toys in the universe. She wanted more puppies so she collected three toys -- a Santa Claus, a little gorilla, a colorful stuffed spider -- brought them into her box, piled them up with the real puppies, cleaned them, pushed them here and there, often close to her nipples. The real pups were with her, on her, behind her, under her for twenty-four hours. She was alert, eating large quantities of food, drinking plenty of water. Of course, even though we entrusted her pups to her, we counted all the time. Now and then we had to pull one out from behind her. We began by bottle-feeding the pups after they nursed, but it was clear they had no further interest in our formula. Celeste was producing quite enough and the pups were putting on weight. This was the way most dogs behave with litters. Celeste's mother was my breeding and was sent to a farm in Brittany as the foundation bitch for a new kennel. When Celeste was born, she was allowed to run loose as a young puppy. She knew no boundaries. Our pups were simply put into larger and larger containments until they could walk off lead in a pack with a human. Not Celeste. She was very different than the pups who had been raised to adulthood in our kennel.

When we let Celeste out to piddle, she stepped daintily from the box, completed her business outside as quickly as possible. She didn't have to be walked. She couldn't wait to get back to her babies. Even so we took her out on leash just to protect her stitches. But she was in such a hurry to get her business over with and return to her babies, we finally let her go by herself. In the worst weather--blowing snow, screaming winds -- Celeste would run up toward the barn and then climb the slate hill above the barn for her private moments. When she returned, breathless, she would pause, look around the box, touch each puppy nose with her own, counting, I'm sure, and then, satisfied with her inspection, tidy up any puppy poop she could find, and then lay down, stretching out on her side and lifting a foreleg to make her nipples available. If one puppy didn't approach her nipples, she would thrust out a huge paw and roll it in, the puppy squealing with fury. Rarely did she make a mistake. If she did, we were right there to move the pups out of her way, pat her dry, and line the pups up on her nipples. One day, very early, a male puppy crept away from her and headed toward the wall of the box. Celeste watched as he stood, staggered and lifted his tiny tail. Celeste sprang up, went to the wall, sniffed his rear, watched the rest of the procedure, sniffed the amazing results of the procedure, lay down again. When he returned to his mother's orbit, she cleaned his rear end, then his face, then everything, rolling him over with alarming force to get to the parts she needed to get to. I could guess what she was thinking: "These are some very interesting toys they've given me. Most of the time my toys just squeak and come apart and leave fluff on the floor. But these things MOVE!" I watched Celeste stir from a deep and snoring sleep, stand, pick up a wandering puppy in her mouth, gently move it back into her space. If a pup had tunneled under a blanket or somehow stuck behind her, she was uneasy; she would scratch at the blanket and alert us that she was missing a puppy. Celeste seemed to know how many puppies she had. Was this possible? Had Celeste really been counting her puppies?

I remember reading that a zookeeper in Toronto discovered that her gorillas could count. The gorilla and keeper were working on an experiment that involved finding raisins under seven paper cups. Only four cups had raisins. The gorilla soon learned that once she hit four cups filled with raisins, there would be no more raisins and no point searching any further. She could certainly count to four. I think Celeste could count. Or perhaps she could just recognize more or less, something is missing. Another zoo keeper in the Lincoln Park Zoo in Chicago reported that one of her gorillas was throwing stones at visitors. The zookeeper offered a grape in exchange for a stone. The gorilla gave her the stone and took the grape. After a number of single exchanges -- if you want this grape, you'll have to give me your stone -- the keeper offered the gorilla the bunch of grapes and the gorilla gave back a bunch of stones. The gorilla at least understood the difference between mass and singularity, of one and many. Of course some gorillas take to throwing feces at their visitors so I don't know how *that* exchange is measured. Exchange may have been diet dependent. At any rate, it might be that Celeste can at the least measure mass. A quick glance told her that all of the puppies were present and accounted for. Did she count? I honestly think she could.

But is animal motherhood truly an instinctive toggle button? Mechanical? Hormones on? Hormones off? At my younger daughter's home in the Vermont mountains a herd of cows arrived in her driveway one sunlit afternoon. Twenty? Two-dozen? Not a herd, a squadron. They were on a mission. They arrived in a row, as cows do, boldly determined about something. They wandered around, poked here and there, in the bushes, behind the trees, behind the shed, and kept looking. They were not grazing. There was something both confused and desperate about their movement. At last, the farmer arriving with two friends, managed to shoo the mothers down the driveway into the road toward home. Their babies, their calves, had been taken away from them which was why they had left the barn. They were looking for their babies: an army of justifiably worried perhaps even heart-broken mothers storming the neighborhood. The story broke my heart as well. How can we dismiss their actions as instinct? They had escaped from their farm a half mile down the road because their children were missing.

A vet from Cornell emailed me a video of an elephant birth in a zoo in Germany. I ached with the elephant's pain as her water broke, gushing out on the floor in a great powerful stream. She flung her trunk over her head and opened her mouth in a silent scream. (There was no sound; I just assumed.) And the baby fell to the floor. It was still born. The elephant kicked it. Then, getting no response, kicked it again and again and then curled her trunk around it, lifted it into the air and swung it and swung it and swung it, just as we had swung our puppies. Finally, the baby must have breathed because the mother laid him on the floor. She fully understood that the baby was alright. She stepped away, returned, pushed it up until it was upright, shoved gently until it walked forward. No one can say instinct about that elephant. She understood exactly what was going on and what she had to do and did it. Not hormones, not instinct -- sheer intelligence, from diagnosis to problem to solution.

During the days and nights with the puppies, I thought about maternal instinct. When women have babies, the act is seen as something close to saintliness. When animals have babies, well, that's just natural, instinctive. The general opinion is that their maternal drive is merely hormonal and has nothing to do with higher feelings since animals are lesser beings than us. I don't think of my dogs as lesser beings. I thought about Julia the gorilla beating her chest with joy when she saw her baby gorilla. Even with dogs,

116

more intelligent than the cows, less than the gorilla, it is, for me, not reasonable, to dismiss the activities of motherhood as mere obedience to our hormones, the hormones of lesser beings. Canine motherhood is far and above instinct. These births weren't all about simple, instinctive, mechanical reactions. If the response to motherhood were merely hormonal, why would it so vary? Personally, I happily managed to snag baby nurses for at least six weeks when my children were born.

One afternoon, clean snow on the ground, a picture post-card day, I took Elsa outside to piddle. In the snow, I could see that her urine was tinged with green. No matter what, she had to go on antibiotics immediately. Antibiotics in her milk would unbalance the pup's digestive system. We were just getting good, ambitious stools. Now we would have a problem. But I had to help Elsa. I had no choice. She had a urinary tract infection aside from the reaction to the anesthesia. Yet another task to write in the log book. And then her milk, which we checked often, turned from creamy pale yellow to green. Elsa had mastitis, a milk infection. I've seen many a dog lose their immune protection because of stress. Certainly Elsa had stress. Fortunately only two nipples were infected. We had to empty those nipples until the milk came out the right color. Elsa would dutifully climb on a platform next to the dogs' bathtub, stand up, and allow us to squeeze her nipples in order to express the infected milk. Since our fingers had no teeth, she allowed us to touch her nipples. It was the puppies she couldn't tolerate. We were welcome.

Because we were sleep-deprived, flooded with coffee and sugar and Hershey Kisses, everything was funny. Even if it was horrible, it was funny. Mamie was bending down on one side of Elsa as I expressed a nipple on the other side. Unintentionally, the milk hit Mamie in the face. She grinned.

The challenge was on. Ready, aim, fire. Naughty grandmothers, we checked Elsa's milk often, maybe too often. We had gone silly, really silly. Most of the nipples had good milk, but, in order to keep the pups off the two infected nipples, we now were forced to control the puppies. After a few even busier days the milk cleared up and we could allow the puppies full access to Elsa's nipples.

Elsa closed her eyes when the pups were nursing. In pain? Celeste would sigh when her puppies were lined up, sigh deeply, close her eyes, and go off to some kind of dog ecstasy. I don't know where Elsa went off to when she was nursing. I think, knowing everything else about her, she simply shut down. One night when she was nursing and two other people were sitting with her to move the puppies around and keep her in place, I was bottle-feeding. I needed to reheat the formula and stood to leave. Elsa shot up, dropped her pups, leaped to follow me. Not pain, the realization hit me over the head. It was fear. Elsa was frightened. I'd used the world overwhelmed; blamed her lack of puppy passion on a lack of instincts. No, she was frightened. All of the other reasons I'd described may have been true but until I had that word on my tongue – frightened-- I didn't understand how truly brave and good she was trying to be. I sent someone else to the kitchen to heat the formula and sat next to Elsa where she could see me. Without a command, she lay down and waited patiently as I put the puppies on. She was being brave. For me. With me. Poor soul, she was trying to be a good dog and it was very difficult because she was already too good a human.

Elsa's pups now slept three and almost four hours between feedings which should have given us a break. But no, keeping them clean, keeping them fed, keeping their space clean was a full time job for all of us. Soon we succeeded in only three feedings a night: at seven, eleven and three a.m. –

not offering them bottles until everyone was really crying. I never left the room. Joyce Red Hat was very competent, but neither Mamie or I could sleep as Joyce talked non-stop through the night. Now we no longer leaped to feed them at a whimper. We let them go as long as possible during the nights. Hungry whimpering didn't count; angry screaming did. We changed the blankets, washed the worst of the puppies off, and prepared more formula, left everything in order for the next shift. Elsa's pups were well underway. Elsa spent her time safe in her own run or attached to me.

CHAPTER FIFTEEN

The next weeks passed quickly although the hours did not. I left pages of notes, of course, because the entire system was in a constant state of flux. Routines lasted a few days and then suddenly amounts, times, directions had to be changed.

Elsa's urinary tract infection retreated. The puppies' bowels were stabilized. Elsa's nipples filled with healthy, creamy milk. Whatever gasses and acids lingered from the anesthesia were expressed. We fed Elsa probiotics daily. At last she began to tell me more often that she was hungry by licking her lips, not actually licking her lips but making one swipe across her mouth with her mighty tongue. That's the signal: feed me.

And she did begin to eat and drink, not with great vigor, but enough to support herself. We offered her scrambled eggs, turkey, chicken and a vast collection of out of date Entenmann's mini bagels, plain donuts, flat breads, sugar donuts from a discount bakery, the chocolate-covered donuts having been set aside for ourselves. Corn Toasties with a spread of peanut butter worked. But if they worked on Tuesday, they might be totally unacceptable on Wednesday; then we brought in cream cheese. Grandma Katie hung out, not only out of curiosity, but for the refused foods. Grass-fed beef liver and assorted organs from the local slaughterhouse worked. Elsa's belly felt softer to the touch, but it was still swollen. She began to greet me with her tail wag when I arrived at her kennel gate to take her to her puppies. A tail wag isn't a sign of pleasure. It's an invitation. I harbored uneasily the feeling she wanted me and no one else with her, but I was too busy to cater to that kind of neurotic behavior. I had hired plenty of people and I deserved some time off myself. No. Elsa communicated to me, somehow, that she wanted me to stay. It was the way she looked in my eyes. I sat on the sofa more often. My back was hurting from bending over the puppies, but I could sit on the sofa and bottle-feed. She liked that. She'd lift her big head, see that I was in place, and then drop her head, and let the pups nurse and the other women move them around. One morning she asked for the bagel I was eating. Asking means putting her face into mine, licking her lips, staring fixedly at the bagel, trying to levitate the bagel into her mouth. I broke off a bit and she buried it in the sofa pillows behind me. That was interesting. When I lifted the pillow I found small piles of Cheezits, a quarter of a peanut butter sandwich, a greenish hunk of liver, and half a Corn Toastie. Elsa was doing what Joy was doing under the bed upstairs: storing food in case of emergency, not her emergency, but for the puppies. She began to show other signs of mothering. I found a whole-wheat mini bagel in the puppies' whelping box. She wasn't hiding that one. She was trying to feed them. She couldn't stand nursing, but she knew they needed to be fed. She didn't trust us entirely. She was moving into acceptable dog behavior, acting normally, accepting her dual nature. But it should be remembered that I now sat with her much more than I had initially, hoping to alleviate the fear.

There were a few emergencies: a puppy who seemed to nurse too long actually wasn't getting enough milk. He would fall off the nipple, not full as we thought, but exhausted. Again someone tripped and fell on a puppy. The puppy revived quickly with a lot or shaking and a syringe of sugar water. A lethargic puppy had dehydrated, refused fluids, and was rushed to the vet for hydration. The little dehydrated pup was marked for special attention, plenty of Pedialyte, and extra bottle feedings. The two underweight girls were thriving. They hadn't gained as much weight as their siblings but they were gaining steadily. They would catch up.

One constant issue was plumbing. At times the pups were constipated; at times, normal, at other times their stool was loose. We swung back and forth with the changes from increasing and decreasing the proportions of liquid to formula powder. We shifted from goat's milk to cow milk. And back. Kerry Brown and his technicians assured us that as soon as they had cereal their guts would stabilize. Bob took to scraping waste off the blankets before he washed them. We noted every poop and non-poop.

And then at long last, they were three weeks old and it was time for cereal. It was time for them to learn eating. In anticipation of the momentous shift from sucking to lapping to eating, three round saucer bowls with raised centers were filled with water and placed around the whelping box and the attached x-pen. The saucers were much like bundt cake pans except the center island was much wider and the surrounding tunnel not as deep. With the island in the center, the pups couldn't wander around in the pan. And they wouldn't be eating and drinking nose to nose.

Litters ago I watched television while I watched puppies. My favorite show, probably my only show, was Teletubbies. Which is why I have a girl I named Laalaa after the female star of the show. Teletubbies were round little happy innocent creatures who lived in a paradise setting with flowers and bunny rabbits and forever blue skies and said, "Uh oh" most of the time. I loved the show because every moment was one of discovery. "Uh oh. A puddle." "Uh oh, a box. What is a box? What do you do with a box?" "Uh oh, put things in the box. Climb in the box." Everything was new and fresh and wonderful. And, as I watched, charmed, I saw the world anew as they did. In Buddhist teaching seeing the world anew is called beginner's mind: a goal. So my little dog Teletubbies with their beginner's minds discovered water. "Uh oh, what's water?" "Uh oh, what do we do with this?" Staggering discovery. And stagger they did, falling into it, out of it, leaping backward in surprise, attacking it again,

122

discovering water. They smelled it. They chewed on the metal of the bowl. They put one paw, both paws, all paws in it. They dunked their heads in it, shook the water off mightily. They ran laps in the shiny tunnel, splashing water everywhere as they orbited. Put your tongue in and drink, little darlings. Sometimes they lay in it; sometimes, I'm afraid, they relieved themselves in it. And sometimes they slept in it, tucked into the puddles and curves, cool and comfy. And finally, one after the other, they put their tongues in it and there it was: the wonder of water. There are many things to do with water but a really good thing is drinking.

The stage was set for eating real food. While the pups' discovery and exploration of water had been hesitant, timid, gentle, the approach to food was a display of nature red in tooth and claw, a ruthless, savage survival drive, wild in every way. I have to admit I'd forgotten what a frenzy it would be. Everyone in the house crowded into the narrow kitchen to watch the triumph, the life-changing, comic, adorable, momentous, momentously messy event. No one wanted to miss this.

On the kitchen counter: a bath mat to keep little feet from sliding, custard cups, a pitcher filled with a mix of formula and Gerber's Baby Stage One rice cereal, a large deep stainless steel pan , and Ms. Pink. With one hand I held her on the counter. With the other I held the custard cup and moved it under her nose. "Uh oh!" Ms. Pink smelled the food, caught me unprepared, leaped from my hand, rocketed herself to the cup. Over went the custard cup. Wipe it up, try again. Oops. She sucked cereal. Bad news. Doesn't work. Her face was already smeared with cereal, ears, nostrils, neck. This second attempt took two of us, one to hold the puppy, the other to hold the custard cup under her nose and direct her head. I put my finger into the cereal, held it up to her nose. She licked it. Then I dropped the finger into the cup. As I had hoped, she followed it down. She forgot lapping and started to suckle again. Suddenly cereal was coming out of her nose. Try again, slowly. This time she tried biting. She bit the edge of the cup. No, wipe her off and start again. She was getting too frustrated and too excited. Another try with the finger and this time, having tried all of her tricks, she licked and lapped, and in a few seconds, she understood. She was lapping up the weak formula/cereal. Ms. Pink was on food. She had invented eating. She went down to the bottom of the custard cup. It was momentous.

The extraordinary scientist Gregory Bateson who studied dolphins made a breakthrough with one dolphin. Offering her a fish, she offered him one learned trick after another but earned no fish. He waited. She went through her routine of trick for fish again, everything she had been taught. But, still, no fish. No fish; the tricks didn't work. At last the dolphin understood. Create a trick. He wanted something new. She offered him a new trick, not one he'd taught her. He gave her the fish. She had taken learning to a new level, the level of invention.

All seventeen pups invented eating for themselves. Some were hesitant, some totally confused, backed away. Some I helped by just dunking their heads into the mix so they at least absorbed a little taste and texture. This was probably stupid to do, but I was so anxious to show them food. For some the custard cup was environment. For some, nourishment. For all, adventure. They were covered. They squirmed, they fought, they slipped, they slid, they threw their faces into the gruel, came out dripping, sneezing, snorting. They were too excited to follow the finger into the bowl, too excited to stay in one place. Most got it after a few tries. Those that hadn't caught on would try again in the evening.

We ordered up another seventeen yarn necklaces. We bathed seventeen pups in the sink. Another four thousand towels went into the washing machine. No matter how vigorously we washed them, as soon as they were back in their puppy space, everyone else was licking them clean, more at the level of molesting them clean. Their ears, which had dipped into the cereal, were the most attractive of targets. Not only had the puppies been covered and grown crusty, but I had cereal up to my elbows. The next day we thickened the gruel slightly and fed them in the evening. They fell down on their full bellies and slept through the night.

Out of the individual custard cups and into the communal saucers. In a few days the saucer bowls that had held water were now filled with the creamy formula, made thicker and thicker each time. The puppies would surround it, orbit it, find their place, and eat. Some would walk in it. Some would lie in it. We hovered over them, lifting them, placing them in vacant spots. We had three saucer bowls going. Six puppies on one, six on the other, five on the third. And then none on this and eleven on this one and then two on that one and seventeen on…

This communal feeding demanded a lot of hands-on effort. Who ate? Who didn't get enough? Who is getting too much? Who's choking? They would run back and forth. Some would stand away, waiting or confused, not wishing to compete. The little girl who would become Lucy was shy, intimidated. We would place her in a vacant space where there was still cereal and keep the pushers away from her. These are the moments you watch for: personalities displaying. Who's the bully? Who's aggressive? Who's timid? It was always Dozer, Mr. Yellow, pushing his siblings out of his way. When all the well-behaved puppies were outside the saucer with their heads down eating, Dozer would climb into the saucer, bulldoze through the cereal, gobbling as he orbited the center island, bumping his siblings out yet again. First he'd bumped them from Elsa's nipples; now from the food bowls. To protect the meek and the small, we'd lift them out of the melee and give them a meal of their own. When tummies were fat and round, the pups went into laundry baskets until all the eating was over. When it was all over – and it was over very very quickly–they were then, yet again, cleaned up. More towels. More blankets. The transition was made. They were eating on their own. From the thin gruel, we progressed daily until we were able to soak real kibble, pulverize it in a food processor, add it to the formula and cereal, and then gradually withdraw the formula altogether. Every day was different with new demands, new instructions, new rules. Mornings when they were sleeping, we'd tiptoe into the kitchen to prepare the cereal. The slightest nick of a spoon against metal had them up and screaming. How fast they learned.

People always say, "Oh, they're so cute. How can you give them up?" That concept of giving them up to other caretakers was becoming more attractive every day. We worked on our hands and knees, the pups molesting us viciously. I often dragged a puppy around on the hem of my nightgown. I graduated into street wear. There was too much company and too much dirty work to wear the nightgowns that swept the floor. When the kennels really had to be torn apart for disinfecting, we let pups loose in the room which meant we then had to clean the room as well.

The pups began with one thin gruel meal a day, then two, then three. We always let them nurse on Elsa but I fed them cereal first so they wouldn't attack her. I brought her in to the pups for the first meal of the day and the last for nursing which she allowed dutifully but she watched for the slightest signal from us that she was finished. She no longer hid or had to be dragged. She trotted alongside me to the puppies, lay down at our command, rolled over on her side at our command, and lifted her leg to offer better access to the puppies. She never took her eyes off me. Very soon she had learned this protocol and reasonably carried it out sans command. This was progress.

Even though, I assumed, her instincts had been atrophied, she so tried to be cooperative, to partner with us, to do what I wanted. It wasn't about the puppies; it was about me, about us. I was always thrilled when she lifted her leg to let the puppies in. We were doing this together. She understood that. I helped her. She helped us. Even so, she hated the sharp-toothed, needle-clawed Lilliputian invasion. Soon she began to lift a back leg when she understood the puppies preferred the lower nipples. Elsa figured out that sitting up to nurse hurts less. Nursing hurt. When it was too painful she stood up which was how they learned to stretch and hang on, balancing on their rear legs to pull on her poor nipples. Then she'd look at me over her shoulder, tell me something, shake the pups off, and dash from the room. I know what she was telling me. "I can't do this much longer." For another two weeks the puppies ate cereal and nursed. Elsa was gradually decommissioned. Celeste had insisted on nursing her babies until they were nine weeks old. We finally had to separate her from her pups. Not so with Elsa. Sometimes she'd race in to see them and then crash into furniture to get out of the room. She was torn.

Elsa's truly profound and natural dog behavior presented itself at four weeks. Unlike her past culinary history, she astonishing us by wolfing down a good three cups of egg noodles and meatballs, stepped without coaxing or command into the whelping box, and dutifully vomited her pile of noodles in front of the hugely interested pups. The pile was gone in a flash. I waited for the meatballs. They were not forthcoming. Houdini-like she'd somehow kept them for herself. How she separated the meatballs from the noodles while they were together in her gut, I will never understand nor certainly emulate. Her message sent "Look, Rhoda, my puppies are ready for real food and I no longer wish to nurse," she jumped over the fencing, curled up on the sofa, and went to sleep. She'd done her dog work. How odd I had to help her be a dog after spending so many years teaching her to be human.

Bob went to town to buy more balls of wool, hit the craft shops for new colors. For me, any reference to the seductive novel <u>Fifty Shades of Grey</u> means soiled puppy collars. I don't know how many times we changed their yarn necklaces. We were beginning, however, to distinguish them by their markings if they would only stand still. Joy learned the markings best. We called out often, "Joy, which one is this? Did this one eat? This one lost its ribbon. Joy, Joy." She was a jumping-jack for us all. Joy had to study for a test of canine structure which I was to monitor and report her grade back to school. She knew our dogs so intimately. To have her point out the names of parts on her test paper seemed infantile. She already knew so much, had learned so much. She nailed the test. And Mamie somehow managed to take a day off and go Christmas shopping—retail! Both Mamie and Joy were making a lot of money on this round-the-clock job. I was not.

For all of us there was no other world than the puppy world. News was limited to who took their Maalox, who ate, who didn't, who needed Gas X, who had a bath, what time they ate, when they needed to eat again, who didn't eat much, who ate too much, and who's coming to visit. That was our world. Oh, and what did the visitors bring for us to eat? Elsa's puppies, now four weeks old, were just too cute, delicious little FAO Schwartz stuffed toys running, jumping, fighting, experiencing, experimenting, watching us, aware. I loved the moment when they fell asleep, one by one, like many plums dropping from a tree, often into Joy's lap.

We had a stream of puppy buyers, friends, people who showed up whom we didn't know, who'd heard about the puppies, seen them on You Tube, read about them in the newspaper. Dave Hamlin, the town supervisor and heroic designated driver after Elsa's C-section, announced at the town board meeting that Port Crane had achieved national attention. So many visitors and all came with food – Chinese take-outs, pizza's, homemade casseroles, country comfort foods, treats for the dogs. The pups were featured in the local paper. While we were more than grateful for any help we could get, we really didn't want visitors but when they came we had them dip their feet in Parvocide or bleach or take off their shoes. If they wanted to hold a puppy, they had to change into one of my unlovely nightgowns. Spray bottles of hand sanitizer were everywhere.

It was hard to believe that in another two weeks Elsa's pups would be six weeks old and ready to go back to Kerry Brown for their first exam and parvo vaccination. Then they would go to Cornell for a cardiology clearance. And in a month more, they would go to their new homes. Again, too fast and yet not fast enough.

CHAPTER SIXTEEN

With so many helpers and so many ever-shifting protocols, it was not surprising we would make mistakes -- a kennel door left open, a chain unhooked. One morning Elsa was feeding her pups. Eight pups were with her. A fence divided the others from her. We watched her carefully. She might allow them to nurse for a few minutes and then she'd flee to the gate and try to escape. If she escaped, they escaped so we had to be ready for her. This morning she sat up while they nursed; she seemed calm. Celeste, on her way outside for her morning walk, took a sudden turn, raced into the puppy room, leaped into the center of their run, breaking down the divider and releasing the other half of the puppies. It was the moment I had most feared. I was ready for blood. I was about to leap in and grab Celeste by the collar. I thought better of it. My action and my terror might precipitate other actions from them. I shouted for help.

Since they were yearlings, there has always been something uneasy, something unsettled, between Elsa and Celeste. Celeste and her brother Theo played wildly, racing in circles, leaping in the air, crashing mid-air into each other. One morning Celeste made the tactical error of backing up as Theo approached and she crashed into Elsa who reacted with anger. To me, it was clearly an accident, but not for Elsa. She may have been insulted. She also may have simply determined that Theo and Celeste were fighting and they were not supposed to fight. With a lion roar, she attacked Celeste. Celeste, an instinctually wild girl much less humanized than Elsa, was more than willing to fight back. When bitches fight, it is said (but thank God I've never seen it), they fight to the death. It took three of us to pull them apart. Elsa had Celeste's ear; Celeste had Elsa's throat. We pulled at their tails, legs, rib cages to no avail. Finally, in mixed company, we tore off our t-shirts and covered the girls' eyes. The brief second of surprise allowed us to separate them and drag them into their separate kennels. Celeste must have said, "I was only playing. I didn't mean to bump into you." Elsa must have said…and she did as I called the animal communicator to speak with them: "Celeste doesn't follow the rules." "Who makes the rules, Elsa?" I asked. Without hesitation Elsa's reply through Mary Long's ether was, "I do." I still think Elsa made an error in judgment, that Celeste had no intention of hurting her. There just wasn't any time for a placating play bow signal. But that's who Elsa is. She makes the righteous rules. I thought I made the rules, but there is an entire handbook that the dogs have to which I am not privy. Now that she's matured I have witnessed Elsa ruling. When Theo, her father who is far larger than she and much stronger, decides to have a noisy conversation with another male who is secure behind a fence, Elsa moves right in, grabs him by the ear, and pulls him away from the fence, quite righteously so, and hustles him back to his kennel. That's a rule: we are not supposed to fight. Elsa stops fight. I would venture that it is a rule she learned from us and not one she inherited genetically. Celeste, on the other hand, is quick to anger, willing to fight. In the wild, bitches will steal pups. Bitches will kill each other. And Celeste has that streak of wildness within her. With Celeste entering this sanctified and dangerous territory of Elsa's whelping box, I didn't know what would happen. Would they fight? Tear a puppy apart? Anything was possible.

Fortunately self-righteous Elsa made a new set of rules, then and there. Elsa continued to sit quite placidly with her puppies under the belly where the richest nipples were. The puppies charged Celeste, attached themselves viciously to Celeste's empty nipples, and went to work. Celeste sat patiently, serenely. Although she had no milk, her nipples were still elongated from her last litter. There, in one kennel, with seventeen voracious pups, the two mothers sat side by side while the puppies nursed, hanging off one nipple here and one nipple there, running back and forth, double-dipping between the multitude of marvelous faucets, leaping and stretching to catch a nipple on high.

Because we really didn't know what Elsa would do, what move might trigger fear, anger, or a bloody tug of war, we scrambled to save the puppies, and remove them from Celeste. It was impossible. We shouted for more help, separated the puppies, and finally dragged Celeste out for her morning walk with one enthusiastic puppy still dangling from Celeste's nipple, little legs churning the air. The suction is so powerful I always think the dog is going to lose a nipple. Finally, Elsa went off to the peace of her own kennel, and, hands shaking, we examined all the pups for wounds. They were fine. I had expected disaster. I should have given the mothers more credit. I imagined Elsa communicated in her dog telepathy, "Hey, Celeste, I could use a little help here." And Celeste responded. "Don't mind if I do. Love puppies. Miss my own." Elsa had drafted a new set of rules, rules, I daresay, very much like my own. Peace, kindness, obedience, trust, and sharing. More cautionary notes and exclamation points in the log book although none of us would likely forget what might have happened. Put all dogs on leads when you take them out of their runs and when you bring them back into the house. Count puppies. Count puppies.

The puppies needed more space. Their whelping box and extension in the office were far too dense. And they had to learn indoors versus outdoors. Out of the comfort of their office, the familiarity of the whelping box, we moved them into a long concrete room at the end of the basement which had an indoor-outdoor kennel. Now they could see what was happening outside the wooden walls of their first home. Now they could run. To the new kennel, we attached two lengths of x-pens to the opening. That added another ten square feet. Attaching the light-framed exercise pens to the fixed and heavy frames of the runs was no easy task. And the Rube Goldberg assortment of bungees, concrete foundation blocks, two by fours, and heavy clips was tough to manage. Complex as it was, Elsa's pups now had a six by six indoor area attached to the ten by ten x-pen run and, one sunny day very soon, since they now had enough coat, they would be allowed out the door of the central area to outside, to the world. Not yet. It was still too cold outside.

In their new spaces, Elsa's pups had determined that they would eat and sleep within the area of the x-pens and poop in the indoor run. Hopefully, when the door to the outside run opened, they would get the message: you don't poop where you eat and certainly not where you sleep. From that enclosed outdoor space, we added a strong portable kennel which would eventually allow them another ten feet in the open air. All in all, they would have plenty of room with these four spaces.

Elsa's pups exulted in their new freedom. They used every inch of it, running, racing, leaping, rolling, spreading out to sleep. The surrogate mothers were gone, stored for the next litter. The pups exploded into their new spaces. They were filled with energy, gaining weight, thriving, learning, watching us, blooming. And we couldn't stop watching them.

I hung over that x-pen for hours. Their activity looked cute and puppyish to us but in reality their dog natures were unfolding. They had to cross six-million years, give or take, to become our companions. There was so much interaction now. The pups approached each other in leaps and attacked, growling, barking. These were real fights but utterly unprovoked. One split second and the ten second fight-to-the-death was no longer of interest. They chased each other. They flung themselves at us when we sang out "Come, puppy, come." Hearing our sounds, footsteps, conversations, they cried and carried on because, if nothing else, we meant food. What are you thinking, guys? Probably nothing more than "when's lunch?" They were constantly inventing and discovering themselves and each other. "Listen. Did you hear that? I think I just barked." They were rehearsing "dog". But they were also thinking and listening and watching our every move, shaping themselves to each other, shaping themselves to us, whatever we were: those large animals who bring food and water, pick us up, scrub us, rub us, bug us when we're so busy. Within a minute or two of cuddling and tummy-rubbing they were struggling out of our arms and off for new adventures.

Finally on a sunny afternoon I took four roasting pans filled with ground breakfast soaked in liver juices and set them in the snow in the outdoor run. I saw no fox foot prints anywhere, decided Vicky was hibernating. I don't think the pups noticed the snow. They cleaned the pans, raced back and forth from one pan to the other, and then ate snow. But then, one after the other, they moved toward the far wall of the fencing and looked. Looked at the sky, at the trees, at the pond, at the world. They stood still much the way they froze when they first heard music. Now they saw the world. It was, I know, momentous. But then everything was momentous. Uh oh, the world! Uh oh, trees. Uh oh, sky. What a joy to be a puppy and see everything just as it is. Watching them, I also felt their Uh oh, saw things anew. First I imagined their feelings; then their feelings oddly became mine. Oh oh, what a wonderful world. It was poetry.

A month earlier, they were unable to withstand chill, to find food, to eliminate. Now they were attack dogs, rambunctious, and utterly without manners. We were the Gullivers; they the Lilliputians with needle teeth. Going into the kennel to clean, refill the water bowls, replace soiled blankets, manage feeding (deliver, monitor, and pick up pans) meant the puppies had to be out of their space and loose in the room. There, on the concrete floor they disappeared under shelves, under the raised bathtub, into closet spaces. We would collect them, lose some as we opened the gate to stuff the vagrants into their run, count, and then we would go hunting on hands and knees for the strays.

When we tried to clean their runs or manage their eating – sharing food was a tough concept for them – they grabbed the hems of our pants, tore holes with their needle teeth, fixed us in place by hanging onto our shoelaces, our socks, our anything they could nail. The x- pen containments were still tentative, unstable. Bricks and clips and bungee cords hardly increased stability against the mass of puppies. One section of the pen had a knee-high gate, too high to step over – for me – and too small for a human to crawl through. In order to get into the space, we had to undo Bob's Rube Goldberg arrangement of clips and bungee cords which tentatively attached the light-weight pen to the strong permanent walls of the runs. The challenge of taking out one puppy for weighing or washing was awesome. We shoved them back in with our feet, our hands, bumped many a baby nose. Sometimes, when no one else was looking, I caught one and shoved him into the oncoming troops like a battering ram. Joy, young and agile, managed much better than I did to catch and contain.

My trick was to toss handfuls of kibble in to distract them, to divert them away from the gate. Sometimes it was a three-lady process. One of us would lady the gate. The other would stand at the opposite end of the gate and tap on metal (as if it were the roasting pan of food or fill a container with kibble and shake it noisily to trick them into running away from the gate toward the sound of food. Then the lady at the gate would undo the rickety arrangement, step through, pluck up the one we wanted, hand it quickly to the third of the team waiting on the outside and get out as soon as possible before the pups figured out what was happening. Seventeen wild and wooly pups – the least of which weighed ten pounds – meant as much as two hundred pounds on the way, barreling toward us. The gates could not withstand the mass. It was, however, great fun to run around and catch them. "Puppies are loose. Puppies are loose." Everyone came down to help in the hunt. If I had more runs in the basement I would have separated them, but all the runs were taken up with the older dogs. The puppies' run was the largest. More bungees, more clips, more bricks.

We plugged up an old double sink on the floor to serve as water bowl. Because it multi-tasked as toilet and swimming pool, it had to be cleaned and refilled throughout the day. The roasting pans had to be placed in the area carefully, leaving some distance from one to the other, four times a day. Blankets had to be changed again and again. I was caught tossing a clean blanket over a dirty one because I was unable or too lazy to get them all off the blanket in place. And we had to go in to manage, sort of, the food frenzy. We had no idea if everyone was getting enough to eat. Mr. Yellow's (nee Bulldozer) knees were noticeably knobby which meant he was eating too much and growing too quickly. We finally gave up and fed him in a separate crate, not only to limit his food intake but to make certain there was enough left in the pan for everyone else. Mr. Dark Blue gobbled, inhaled. Mr. Red ate slowly and steadily. Mr. Blue would invariably shove his big bony face into Mr. Red's bowl. Mr. Red didn't even lift his head to defend his dinner. He simply swung his head sideways, bit Blue big time on his ankle and, having missed only a mouthful or two, went right back to the business of eating. "No offense, Bro. I just haven't finished yet." Red would grow up to be a good-natured, laid back sweetheart. Blue would be good-natured but quicker, faster, sharper, and continue to steal food from his kennel partner.

Watching those pups as often as we did gave us some accurate predictions. There is a personality test breeders often give at day 49. I gave it for a while to some of my earlier litters. The pup has to go into a strange room with strangers. Does he show fear? The stranger has to squeeze the pup's toe. If he goes to a count of ten, it shows that he doesn't mind being hurt. In other words, how long will he tolerate pain? If you toss a crumpled bit of paper, will he fetch it and bring it back? Some prospective buyers insisted we do this test. Laalaa who turned out to be the smartest dog I've ever had would not go in the room. She knew the people were strangers and she had to watch them for a while. The test might be good for the funny, excited pup that jumps around and will let you hurt him. Okay, he's a good-natured pup. But for a dog who is about to be a saint, who relies on judgment, not power, the ten minute test is ridiculous and the people who call and ask what the puppy's score was…well there are higher requirements in my book. Now that these puppies were watched twenty-four hours a day, we were getting excellent insights on their personalities. Wouldn't it be wonderful to have a camera focused on their prospective buyers?

Some of the pups growled as they ate. This was unacceptable. They had to be separated. The communal feeding became a battle ground. We filled regular single pungent food bowls and, holding the bowls in the air, let half of the pups out of their room. We drummed on their bowls with tablespoons as we marched the pups through the labyrinth, into a hallway, through the office, through the kitchen, into another hallway, into another room where seven or eight crates were set up, shoved two bowls and two pups into each crate, and they ate. No problem, just show us where it is. Now and then one didn't show up, stuck behind a door, confused, disoriented. It was usually one of the Mr. Greens. We had to go back to the beginning, bang on his bowl, and he'd find us. Within two days, they found their way by themselves without the Pied Piper routine, raced through the rooms, stood in front of the crates, and waited for their bowls. Brilliant. At least half of them were getting the right amount of food. We never knew, however, which half. But they were all thriving and their weights were good, except for

Mr. Yellow who weighed six pounds more than Mr. Blue. I had thought about keeping Mr. Yellow. I wasn't sure I could handle a dog as large as he was sure to become. Elsa brought bits of kibble into the puppy's room, dropped them, and ran away. She was so dear, so anxious to be a dog, so afraid. Often she would slink into the puppy room but when the pups saw her and barked and screamed and leaped, she'd run away. So much of her wanted to be a natural mother, but most of her could not. She was too much like us.

CHAPTER SEVENTEEN

Mamie was gone. Her fibromyalgia was kicking up and she hurt all over. Joy returned to school with A's on her report card. Joyce Red Hat was gone. We only needed day time help. The pups were sleeping through the night. They were gorgeous and sweet and totally wonderful. They would start on their vaccination protocol and have heart checks, grow up a little more, and go off to their homes all over the country. I think the appropriate warning here is pride cometh before a fall.

Solomon and I were taking our morning fresh air break when he lifted his head and sniffed the air. Then he trotted over to a creek just across from our driveway at the front of our house. The creek runs into a spring fed stream and then down past our house into a lake. At the juncture of creek and stream he stood wagging his tail at whatever he saw next to the creek. I walked over. A beautiful little fox was lying as if she had fallen asleep in the dead grasses. She showed no signs of damage. She lay easily as if there had been no pain, as if she had died in her sleep. Vicky? Her coat was lovely. She seemed whole and healthy. What kills foxes? Are we all in trouble? Rabies? Lepto? What kind of threatening message is this? I tried to convince myself that this was just a moment in nature, not a message for me. But, paranoid as I had been, I took it as more than a death, a message, a prediction of death.

Either that or a sacrifice.

When they were six weeks old we took them back to Kerry Brown's for their first vaccination. Mary Austin, our kennel manager, who, during the duration of the Newfoundland National Disaster, had been managing the resident dogs, and Bob, and a prospective owner, and I cleaned them up and packed the cars. A very generous soon to be puppy owner, actually insanely generous, came up from Manhattan in a hired dog taxi, cool, handsome driver, and all. I cannot imagine what this utterly first class transportation cost her but it certainly eased the effort. We fitted the city van out with protective flooring, two crates, and stuffed, shoved, pushed, stuffed, shoved, pushed, locked at long last half the puppies in the crates. They carried on. The other half went into two crates in the Suburban. When I climbed into the Manhattan van, the driver handed me a roller to clean the hair from my clothing. First class. I assumed he was being courteous then I realized he was keeping his van clean. From me. So we were off for the two hour each way drive. There was a cacophony of complaints from the rear. The pups were alarmed, but soon the gentle rocking when we hit the highway reminded everyone of that wonderful ride in the paradise of Elsa's grand tummy and they slept. This was a milestone moment.

We used up three rolls of paper toweling and fourteen blankets, some of which we left at the side of the road. Two hours in the car was a challenge. We were met at the vet by five people from the local Newfoundland club, the vet, and the vet techs. There were too many helpers of course and since all the puppies looked so much alike and kept moving around, we had to recheck many of them. Seventeen in a small room. We let some loose who immediately painted the floor. It was intriguing to watch what they did in a new surround. This one was brave; these were fearful. This one was too brave. All of them were picked up and cuddled. The vet was annoyed with us and hushed us as he listened to their hearts. Bob quieted all of us down, found the right colored puppy, scribbled notes. This one had a mild murmur. This one was okay. This one had an extra tooth. Then they received their parvo shots, their first vaccination. There was nothing life-threatening. Maybe the fox's death was not a message at all but simply what happens in the wild. We were not in the wild. Maybe my paranoia was truly misplaced. When the exams were done and Kerry nodded at me and said, "Good job," Bob dropped three beads of a homeopathic remedy to protect the pups from a reaction to the shot. A shot after all is the disease itself: Parvo. It's the first shot they get because that's the disease that most threatens them after their mother's protection system has run out.

Even so, we got it. The fox was right. Parvo is a deadly disease. It usually wipes out half of a litter, sometimes more, sometimes all. Mary Austin stepped out of the vets' office for a cigarette. A woman pulled up, carried a small puppy out of the car and into the Dr. Brown's office, and came right back out. The pup was highly contagious and had to be isolated. She had just picked the puppy up at the airport where it had been shipped to her. It had bloody diarrhea. Which is the first sign of Parvo. She put the puppy down on the ground. Parvo is airborne. Is this where we got it? Just from our shoes? But the ground was frozen. Or did we get it from the shots? Or the crowd of visitors who came for the puppy shower the next week? Or from the shot itself, which sheds in the feces and could be picked up.

It was time for the Cornell cardiology check. I had no idea they were coming down with the disease. They seemed active and had eaten their first meal of the day well. I had had dozens of litters before and never had a disease so I expected nothing. I will never forget that day marching into Cornell with this gorgeous litter of pups. I was so proud. People in the waiting room left their seats and stood in the lobby to watching this marvelous parade of white-coated, stethoscope-draped interns, residents, professors carrying puppies through the lobby. Admiration society beyond beyond. We went into a much too small examination room where a half dozen cardiology interns, residents, and two professors were waiting, some with floor mops. Everyone had a turn examining the pups. Who were examining them, licking, tugging on shoe laces, chewing on power cords, attacking the mops. Except for Mr. Gray who was sleeping under a chair. All the hearts were fine. There were a few juvenile murmurs which would vanish soon enough. But something was terribly wrong with Mr. Gray.

I weighed Mr. Gray as soon as we were home. He had lost weight. We raced down to the local vet for blood work. Parvo takes a week or more from the time of the shot to manifest itself. It was time and it was manifesting. The next day the vet called to say Mr. Gray was positive for Parvo. But Elsa's pups had all had parvo vaccinations. The vaccinations hadn't kicked in. But how did they get the full-blown disease? Weren't they protected? Do foxes carry Parvo? Had the fox brought it to us? Was it from the vaccinations themselves? Was it something on Mary Austin's shoes from the sick puppy outside the vet's office, something deadly that came home with her, something airborne? In the crowd, we just hadn't noticed Mr. Grey's malaise. Perhaps it had just manifested the day we went to Cornell. He was the first to contract it and his disease was light. He was actually over it. He'd been eating and drinking and there was no suspicious diarrhea in the spaces Elsa's puppies occupied or else nobody had noticed it, which was more likely.

When I put down the phone I shook in raw terror. The vet told me the signs and what I should do. I ran to examine whatever stool was on the ground. Some was indeed now loaded with strings of bloody mucous –stomach lining. It was starting. The vet said I would have to turn the kennels into a hospital, an isolation ward. He didn't have enough room in his isolation ward for all the puppies. We would have to disinfect everything, keep the older dogs away from the young ones. Parvo strikes weak immune systems. Why hadn't we noticed? The loose stools were familiar. In healthy pups diarrhea comes and goes as you change formulas, change amounts of food, change the mother's food. But it was easy to control. We just added the Bene-bac gel. As puppies move from mother's milk to soaked food to thick kibble, they do get upset tummies. Diarrhea wasn't an event, just, for us, a signal to give more probiotics. But on really close examination, we found the bloody stools. I remember my face turning beet red. Indeed, by nightfall, more of the puppies had stopped eating and were curled up in painful balls, lethargic, feverish. When that phone call came in from the vet telling me Mr. Gray had tested positive, a family was visiting for the third time to choose their puppy. Mr. Red's owner-to-be was back to check on her choice. And a dear friend, a Newfy owner and trainer himself, had driven the two hours up from Syracuse to celebrate the puppies. There was no celebrating. We piled the worst of the puppies into Gary's car and off they went to Kerry Brown's to go into isolation or death. What had I done? How did this happen? Everything in my heart went with them and yet there was no time. We had to isolate the others. I have never felt such terror in my entire life. Parvo is a horrible disease in which the bacteria eat the stomach lining. The pups die in pain, from starvation, or dehydration. The disease is over quickly. The rate of survival depends on how much damage the disease had done. My babies. Terror was overwhelmed by fury.

We disinfected every inch of their environment with Parvocide. But it was far too late. Some of the pups had stopped eating; some had the bloody stool already. There was nothing to do. Kerry and Frank, his partner vet, called again and again. The pups were on medication. The vets were trying avian flu medicines. They were trying everything. One simply has to get them through it and hope there wasn't too much damage. I dropped 6 cc's of Colloidal silver into the mouths of the older dogs because it is supposed to encapsulate germs. Late that night when there was nothing more to do, I sat at the computer and looked up parvo. In all my years of breeding, I had never experienced an illness of this magnitude in any of my litters.

The first website I pulled up said, in large letters, "Are you sitting by while your puppies die of Parvo?" Yes. "Get this." I called first thing in the morning and ordered overnight shipping for something homeopathic called Parvoguard. It consists of ionic water infused with such things as plantain leaves, jewelberry, and Echinacea. Not so convincing. I called Mamie, begged her to come back and help me. Generously, in spite of the fact that she had just had a Maltese litter of her own, she did. We had to syringe all the puppies every three hours for forty-eight hours with 30 cc's of the Parvoguard. Mamie and the overnight shipment arrived the next morning and we started. Mamie, graciously and with great courage, syringed the Parvoguard, the Pedialyte, baby food when we could, vanilla Ensure when we could, and aloe vera juice because it heals internally.

Every three hours we would sterilize all the syringes, fill them with 30 cc's, wake up the babies, and medicate them. Sometimes Mamie had to wake me up. Sometimes I had to wake her up. It was utterly exhausting. By nightfall all of the puppies at home were up and dancing. It was a miracle. I called Frank to tell him I was bringing the Parvoguard in, that the puppies left at home were all better. He hadn't heard of Parvoguard, but he was more than willing to try anything. Later he called from the hospital. Mr. Purple had died. They were all struggling to survive. The round-the-clock dedicated technicians, garbed in isolation gear, were managing to get some liquid in them. Most of the time the pups threw up anything. Mr. Purple. Oh, God. I had to bury that death in my heart in order to go on. Red was in trouble but holding her own. This one was on the edge. Kerry called every night sometimes more often. He wasn't sure about that one. He had everyone on the net looking for cures. They found some drugs. With half of my Parvoguard supply I drove the hundred miles daily, back and forth, to Kerry's and my babies.

I was allowed to go into the isolation unit. Crates on top of each other, my puppies lethargic and whimpering. They were in agony. Ms. Red, a little black female with her white tail and white paws, wagged her tail. How can I help you? I've taken every one of your beautiful little breaths with you and now I am helpless and you are hurting so terribly. What can I do? They were getting round the clock care and I had to be home for the others and the three hour syringing. There was neither time nor energy for heartbreak.

Gary, our friend who had helped bring them in to Kerry's, shuttled the hundred miles, two hours back and forth, bringing us meds, Parvocide, syringes, intravenous set-ups, and then returning to Kerry's with Parvoguard and aloe vera juice because THEY WERE WORKING. I drove in every evening. Within a few days, Gary began to bring puppies home. It was a week before they all came home. But they weren't at all well. The disease was gone but the damage was considerable, life-threatening. Still very much in danger, they refused to eat or drink, vomited when we force-fed them. They were seriously dehydrated. We set up the intravenous bags on coat racks, learned quickly to insert the syringe and wait for the bubble in the puppy's back when enough liquid had gone into their sweet, pathetic little bodies. They were as thin as baby birds, fragile. One little girl had gone from eleven pounds down to eight. (She's now a champion and a mother.) We had new sets of very serious rules: nobody comes in the room without booties, caps, and scrubs. Change the foot baths. Get more Parvocide for the foot baths. Wash everything every day with Parvocide. Bleach in the laundry.

The isolation room was immaculate. Each sick pup had its own kennel. We had the crates piled double with two on the desk. We changed the bedding endlessly. I was too tired to pray, but I was sure the universe knew what I wanted. Mamie and I didn't sleep for more than a few hours at a time. The syringes had to be sterilized each time. Just Mr. Purple. Poor beautiful Mr. Purple. So far.

I took no phone calls. My theatrical agent called to ask me to write a paragraph about a play that was booked for the summer. I couldn't. Nothing existed but those puppies. They were more active, crying to be released, to be with each other. Finally, if they'd eaten food for a few days and their stools were normal, we took them out of their crates and let two or three play together on the floor for a few very happy moments. They were lonely for each other. Susan's boy came after school. He was a Godsend. He played with the sick puppies, one more each day until all could go on the floor and race around the room. He named the littlest boy Pablo. Pablo had lost hair and was shedding skin. He had been the most damaged. Had been. He was alright. He cried and scratched at his door to be free of his crate. At last we put him on the floor with a little female and they fell on each other. We allowed them a few minutes together. We couldn't crate any of them together because we had to watch their stool output and food and water intake. They yearned for each other.

And then it was over, just as mysteriously and quickly as it had begun. Had it come from a germ from the woman in the parking lot with the sick puppy? From the visitors? No one wore shoes into the house. Had it come from a germ sloughed off in the feces from the vaccination itself? That is my suspicion and, I think, the greater likelihood. They caught it *from* the vaccination. All of the pups went back to Kerry Brown's for check-ups. Pablo needed hair on his shoulder but it was coming. They were fine. And we all shook our heads.

How did we do this? How did we save all but one? We did it by working together. The vets had made me a complete partner. That Elsa produced seventeen puppies was no longer news. Having saved so many very sick puppies from parvo death was news. Curing them with Parvoguard and aloe vera was news. I told every breeder I knew and told them to tell every breeder they knew: keep a supply of Parvoguard handy. Within two weeks, the pups were out of the woods, putting on weight, eating, playing. Whatever is in that Parvoguard --and it is nothing that would impress anyone medically, traditionally trained – it, combined with superb veterinary care, worked for me. However that first ad appeared…are you sitting still while your puppies are dying of parvo…the first thing I saw when I collapsed at the computer, I don't know. But it saved my puppies. Except for dear little Mr. Purple who had to have suffered in an agony I have to bury in my heart. Afterward, long afterward, I allowed myself the heartbreak. It took me over a year to be able to write this chapter. I didn't want to relive those terrible weeks.

Footnote: *When I googled Parvoguard, a message came up from a breeder who had a different experience. She gave her pups Parvoguard and they died immediately. I couldn't find any reference or availability of Parvoguard. Obviously it was taken off the market. The company had disappeared. Since then, it seems to be back on the market, renamed Parvaid.*

CHAPTER EIGHTEEN

And somehow the puppies were eight weeks old. And now, finally, all were out of the isolation room and ready to live it up in their four room kennel space. I think the puppies expanded as soon as they were put into this vast space. Puppies adore new spaces. As soon as they hit a new stretch of flooring, they pee and poop. House training began.

This business of becoming civilized in a human space is a massive leap from the wild to the home. It's a lot to learn. They are born with the knowledge that they cannot pee where they live. That's a plus. Once that knowledge kicked in at a few weeks, they had determined that a particular corner was the space to use. When they moved into their new extensive four section apartment, we had to start all over again. Where do I pee? I can't pee where I live but there are a lot of places I don't live. I can't pee in my run because this is where I live and that's against the dog rules. But I have to pee and either there are other dogs watching me or I can't get outside. So where do I pee? I have to find a new surface other than the one I sleep on. And there are more challenges. If I can't pee where I sleep I have to pee in something that isn't my run and I don't want to go outside or I can't go outside. Oh, look. This double sink filled with water is not my run. It is not what I sleep in. Therefore I can pee in it because it isn't my run and the rule doesn't apply.

The moment they managed to break down the bungee/cord, brick containments, they raced into *our* spaces outside their run and relieved themselves. It's a beginning of toilet training – not-here-where-I-live-but-there-where-I-don't-live. There were far too many puppies all together but I had no other place to put them. With a combined weight of almost three hundred pounds now, they easily knocked the barricades down and were racing around the basement with all of us crawling after them in hidden spaces. And of course, since they were in a new space, they evacuated and ran through their messes, spreading them far and wide. So we were not only up to our ankles and knees, but had pasted souvenirs to our elbows.

We had to open the guillotines often and call them outside. It was still too cold to leave them outside or leave the guillotines open all the time. Bob had built a platform with a few bricks for steps to soften their jump from house to ground. Moments after they ate, I would stand outside and call. "Puppy, Puppy," I called in the high sing-song all mothers keep for babies. One and two and then three crowding, pushing, they came out, rediscovered snow, started to play fight with each other, ran, raced around the space, peed and pooped. Fresh snow is a new surface.

The interface between relieving one's self wherever and whenever you wish and controlling one's furry self until one gets outside is an abyss we all had to cross. Their father, Solomon, following the not-there-where-I-live-but-here-where-I-don't-live rule as a young male devised a method that was both despicable and admirable. He peed in an empty food bowl or a hopefully empty water bucket. I never understood this. Even when his run was open to his outdoor run, he still filled, fastidiously and accurately, the empty bowl or bucket or his sister's food bowl. Watching Solomon's runaway puppies urinate as soon as they hit the concrete floor beyond their confines or the new snow, I realized what Solomon might have thought when he began this habit.

Saint Solomon, even as a pup, came upstairs into our space and was completely respectful of our alpha role and therefore of all the things that belong to us. He would sniff and examine every book, pencil, cup, newspaper, food, scrap of paper, but take nothing. He has a concise map of all of our things. If something has been moved or added, he would inspect it, take note, correct the maps in his head. It is our room, not his. He knows that very well. But he extrapolates from the efficiency and availability of his round and deep and empty food bowl or bucket to the over-indulgent Ralph Lauren hand-tufted leather ottoman in the living room. That ottoman has deep indentations in it, eight of them, with buttons in the bottom of the indent.

At first I thought a visitor, too embarrassed to report it, had spilled a drink into one of the holes -- a coke or a beer they'd rested on the ottoman. But no. For hole number two, we had had no visitors to make such a mistake. And for hole number three, I caught Solomon at it. No dribbles, no spills, entirely intentional, precise. "This is not the room. The ottoman hole is similar in depth and circumference to my water bucket. I don't sleep in this spot. This is something else. I can pee right here." He never pees anywhere else in the house, never marks. I suppose I could follow through with his predilection for deep spaces as pissoirs and lead him to the toilet itself, which somehow reflects the depth and circularity of what he chooses, and, in fact might indicate that he's mirroring our behavior. But no, I'd shared enough with him already and there are still five tufted urinals to go in the ottoman. If the tufted areas all look alike, with deep dark circular stains, perhaps no one will notice.

Our first Rosie (we recycle names) solved the not there but here problem in another way. Until she was too stiff to climb the stairs, she slept in our bedroom every night and would invariably pee directly in front of the toilet bowl.

I remember hiking in Tibet and trying to empty my bladder into a hole in the ground. It was not only a physical but an emotional challenge. I can't. I can't. I must. I remember flying out of Nepal and finding sneaker footprints on the seat of the airplane toilet. Someone clearly Asian had been standing on that toilet, balancing herself in mid-air in order to empty her bladder, which was even more of a challenge because there was nothing in that tiny room to hold onto other than a single light bulb in the ceiling. Culture

150

versus culture. When one of my dogs has an accident, I consider those Nepalese footprints and forgive my babies entirely.

Saint Solomon had somehow worked out a protocol to maneuver the dreadfully confusing interface between where he pees and where we pee, between doing as we do and doing what comes naturally. It was Elsa's dilemma as well. What do dogs do? What do humans do? What do I do? Dogs, for example, clean puppies' bottoms. Humans don't so I don't. To the detriment of her pups, Elsa hadn't balanced these dual demands. Our pets have to operate between their nature and ours and keep their dual nature in balance. Solomon's father, Captain Nemo, was terrified by the shiny surface of his kitchen floor so he figured out how to adapt to the human environment: walk in backwards so you don't have to look at the floor. Bewildered as they must be between doing as we do and following their own anciently wired dog rules, they have to work hard to live in our human world, to obey our rules. How good, how truly good of them to try.

Footnote: As a footnote to this discussion on early toilet training, if anyone doubts that behavior is genetic, Solomon's son Mr. Dark Blue, Ben-to-be, will also make the same decision as to where he can legitimately relieve himself when he can't get outside: water bucket, food bowl, double sink.

CHAPTER NINETEEN

A prospective buyer who owns a training facility visited Elsa's pups weekly. She and her friend would take a puppy out into the office, watch him walk around, judging the movement. They spent hours and hours. And came back again and again trying to decide what that puppy would be like grown, what his movement was like, what his disposition was going to be. It was an impossible task. They would spend four and five hours a day judging. Finally one day, I said, "Just take Mr. Red." Eventually she did. Happily ever after. He became Loki. His American Kennel Club name became Blue Heaven's What Were You Thinking. It was a question she was asking me and most likely what Elsa had been asking me.

I knew what these pups would look like because above their whelping boxes an entire wall was filled with head shots of our dogs, from the beginning -- an honorable wall of ancestors. Once you've seen enough pups mature, it's fairly easy to predict. This pup looks like that dog on the wall looked when he was a pup so this pup will probably look like this one. There are types that turn up in litters, types you've seen before. So, on that singular non-scientific anecdotal theory, in my sleep-deprived hallucinations, I imagined that some non-local energy the ancestors might have would transfer to the puppies in the boxes beneath the wall – a frequency, the Twilight Zone electric energy blueprint. The puppies might just become that venerable ancestor or at least make space in their great souls-to-be for a bit of their marvelous forebears.

I would like to think this transfer has happened before -- a wrinkle in time sense that the ancestor dogs hover, waiting to enter another body. Those into this kind of thinking -- and there are many -- report a suspicion, certainly fueled by a desperate hope that their dead dog has returned. When Mary Long reported that long-gone Ishtar was determined to become the living Bumper and young Bumper said she felt pain but didn't know if it were her pain or someone else's pain, Bumper was experiencing another presence. It seemed to me, I add with hesitation, because if any of this were true we'd have to start that new religion, that Bumper knew there was someone else in some way around her. That she was aware of another dog, not quite present, but even so, present. About that cloud, about Pippa's possible presence at Elsa's delivery -- a close friend's dog, Phineas, who indicated there were other dogs in the house, in spirit. Phineas would take a piece of meat from his dinner bowl, take it to the far end of the kitchen and place it on a dog mat, a dog mat which appeared as an unoccupied dog mat to his owners, but not to Phineas. Then he would return to his mat, his dinner, and sit there watching that piece of meat on the other side of the kitchen. He was waiting for someone, an out-of-the-body altruism. He was leaving that meat for a dog who wasn't there but, just as Pippa's cloud, was there. What/who did Phineas see? Panda and Bou were aunt and niece, both my breeding. Panda raised Bou from puppyhood. They slept in "nests" at the bottom of their owner's bed. When Panda died and did not come home from the vet's, Bou laid a dog biscuit in Panda's empty nest. Was it an invitation? Come back, come back? Was it a gift? Was Panda, in some way, still present for Bou? Unlike Phineas, she did not continue the action: She did it once on that night of Panda's death and never again. What are these dogs thinking? One thing is certain, they are thinking. And above all, feeling.

It's hard to argue with Emma's story. Two litters ago, a couple called for a puppy. The wife is a psychiatrist, the husband an inventor -- not minimal minds, to say the least.

153

They had word from their animal psychic that their recently deceased Newfoundland was to be born again at our house. When the pups arrived, the husband drove eight hours across the country. He called his psychic at midnight and told her he thought he had found Emma. (You see, I'm not the only one.) The psychic confirmed that the puppy he had chosen was indeed Emma. I, of course, tore my hair out. I had my eye on that little girl for myself. One of the prerogatives of breeding is that the breeder gets to pick who gets what puppy. Even so the couple persisted, and, because I liked them, in fact, admired them greatly, I sold them the pup who was to be Emma. As if she had never left, when the new Emma arrived at her home, she went immediately through the front door, into the living room, took a left turn through the kitchen, and out to the sun porch, and onto the sofa, and took her place on that exact pillow where the first Emma always lay. She was completely familiar with the house, with the habits of the old Emma and, as the years passed, would continue to convince her owners -- who needed no convincing -- that she was more than just the new dog in the house.

Among dog persons, these anecdotes are repeated over and over again. Crazy or not, it is comforting to think that a dying dog might actually come back again in another form. Crazy or not, as I hold a dying dog in my arms for those last, terrible, and inevitable moments, I always thank them for their good work and invite them back anytime. "Come back as a puppy. Come back." Our first Molly, years after she passed, said to Mary Long that she didn't want to come back because being a puppy was such hard work. A woman who lost a beloved Golden named Chase reported that her nephew had decided that Chase was inside the Newfy puppy we'd sold her. She thought it was funny. The new puppy immediately found Chase's toys. I think her nephew was correct. Chase was somehow in some ethereal

Solomon the sire.

The litter in the
incubator, just born.

Pippa's cloud,
already breaking up.

Dave Hamlin,
first feeding of new born.

New born in hand.

One day old litter with
surrogate stuffed toy mom.

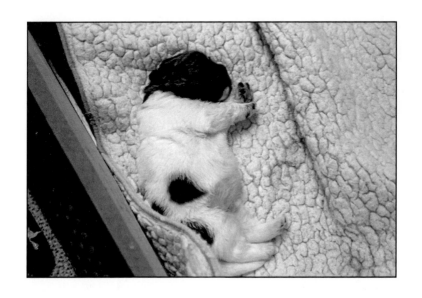

One day old,
couldn't eat a drop more.

Three days old,
can't see; can smell.

Day twelve, can see.
I can see you!

Two weeks. Mr. Yellow,
aka Bulldozer. (Guess why)

Three weeks. Down to the bottom
and all over me.

Cereal was a good idea. I'm getting bigger.

First day in outdoor run.

First walk in the snow.

Getting to be a dog.
Ready to go. I'm serious.

Coco finds her mom, Sally Mabadi.
Mom, Mom, where have you been?

Elsa contemplating life.

Molly, Great Ancestress of us all.
She is the great, great, great, great grandmother
of this litter. Every puppy we have had goes back
to Molly. This is the sixth generation.

Laalaa, Elsa's
and Bumper's mom.

Great, great granddaddy Packard
who loved puppies.

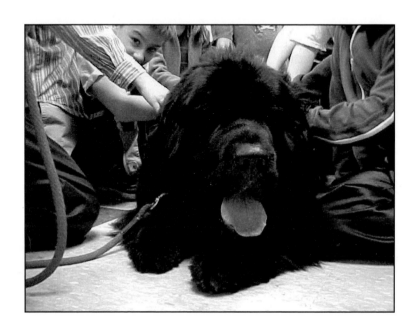

Theo, granddaddy,
Elsa's dad.

Elsa and her shoe habit.

Solomon, pride and joy.

Celeste afloat, the wild child.

Rosie, tidying up the lake.

Four generations: left to right -
Katie, Laalaa, Bumper and baby Rosie.

Elsa chatting with a friend.

One year later, Elsa finally has
her own single puppy to love.

Pippa

I think I may have stepped in something.

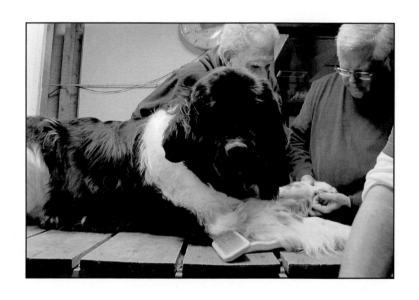

Spa Day

We all would like to come in and join you:
left to right - Bumper, Laalaa and Rosie.

way inside the new puppy-- perhaps just visiting to make certain the new guy had a good start.

Had the old Emma shaped the new Emma? Did Ishtar shape her great- granddaughter Bumper? Did she give her pain? Elsa is so like her grandmother Katie in appearance and actions, when I put my hand out to pat her on the head while I'm writing or watching television, inattentive, I am not sure who I'm petting. I often call Elsa Katie. It is hard to tell the difference. Newest science claims that DNA can be changed in a generation and in moments by particular radio frequencies, as in music. Buddhists say seven generations. Maybe Ishtar was working on the young Bumper. Maybe the ancestors on the wall are working on the puppies. And maybe, just maybe, to take it into the Twilight Zone, my dogs are working on me.

CHAPTER TWENTY

Elsa's puppies were twelve weeks old. They had been examined and re-examined. They were fine. Every time I went back with them to Kerry's, we all hugged and congratulated each other. We had shared a miracle.

By twelve weeks any real physical ailments would have shown up, any behavioral idiosyncrasies would have been identified. By that time, they were generally civilized. They had been leash trained, had names given by their new owners, knew a few commands, ("sit" better than "stay") and, most importantly, "come," which they did more quickly if you had a cookie in hand. They had learned to walk on the trails in a pack off lead. They had been taught how to go up and down a ramp to get into a car. They knew to go outside to relieve themselves, which meant they were house-trained but only to my house. I had full confidence they would extrapolate easily. They knew in and out.

Their owners- to-be came to visit and cuddle. Love and laughter filled the house. Money poured in; poured out faster. The week of intensive care for the parvo hospitalization could have paid for a small car. We were very much in the red, but the house was filled with people, cake, coffee, lunch, soup, overnight guests, pride, and so much love. The new parents came to visit their puppies, carried them upstairs, held them while the rest of us ate and ate and laughed. We make certain new owners visit with the big dogs, get licked, shoved, jumped on, slimed, know what they are getting into. Once in a while one owner's eyes would slide over to another puppy, comparing. But each of the owners had different needs: companion dog, bed pet, show dog, therapy dog. I lectured about the puppy's needs rather than the owner's needs. I was growing anxious. Did the owners know enough? Had they read everything I'd assigned? Had they bought everything on the emergency list? Could they get the special shots we insist on? Did they get the indoor/outdoor carpeting for the hardwood floors? Have they found a proper vet? Getting the puppies ready was almost behind us. Getting the people ready was very current. And kept me up at night.

Every pup was a wonder. Bob and I hugged each other endlessly. As we passed. We were too busy to stop. Our hearts were filled with pride and joy and the sweet sadness of sending the pups off to their lives which was so much like marrying off a daughter. The pups were so ready for love, for attention, for cuddling, for holding. There was no way I could give them the attention they needed. And the poop was monumental.

The pups had an hour a few times a day in a large outdoor run with a shallow muddy stream, melting snow, apple trees, rotten apples, toys, dog houses, and, most importantly, each other. One of us would stand at the gate to the paddock, banging with the tablespoon on the very dented pot. That was the signal. "Come, puppy, come," I would sing. Someone would open their gate at the house. This was the moment of joy. They raced to the paddock, ears flapping, like a school of fish, a single unit. Then they ran in great circles in the paddock, smelling the ground, exploring, chasing, rotten apples in their mouths. I would sit at a picnic table in one of the paddocks and do nothing but watch their joy as they turned into mud puppies. We all kept our eyes open for the fox. Would Vicky or Sly leap the fence and steal a puppy in the way they kill chickens? No one had seen the foxes for a month. Now that the snow was off the ground we had no way of tracking them. Still I left kibble above the barn at the rise where we last saw them, hoping to see them again. But not near my puppies.

Everyone now had been named by their owners-to-be. Noble names, charming names, silly names, loving names.

We had two Sampsons and two Delilahs. They all had people names, Biblical names, not joke names like Tiny or Murphy. Mr. Dark Blue took the triumphant title of them all: Ben, after my first Newfy– my first soul mate. Ben was my keeper.

All the new owners had been warned that I would be their mother-in-law: invasive, critical, but always available. Repeat owners knew I don't let go easily. In fact, I never do. The owners had been beaten over the head with directions, instructions, their own shopping lists, warnings and more warnings. The contracts they'd signed were five single-spaced pages long with legal threats just above the space for signatures. We stood over their shoulders as they read. It was enough to make them paranoid which was just what I wanted.

And then it was time to send them out.

Where were they going? Matchmaker that I tried to be, intuitive, hopeful, suspicious, judgmental, hopeful, always hopeful, I had reviewed the lists of owners and puppies endlessly. I had had no choice about who my children would marry. Not that I didn't have opinions which I had to keep to myself. But I certainly could exercise my opinions in these situations. The executive woman who had her assistant calling us was clearly off the list. Our rule is that hopeful buyers come to our house, no matter how far away they live, so we can meet them and they can meet us and, most particularly, the grown, leaping, sliming, enormous adult dogs. Some prospective owners were folks who had already owned one of our dogs. Some had been waiting for years. ("I breed Arabians. I saw your dog at a show and I know a fine animal when I see one." She had waited three years.) Some we met for the first time, but they'd read my book, In The Company of Newfies, and absolutely had to have a Blue Heaven dog. (When the book went out of print, somebody placed it for sale on EBay for $896.00 and there were crazy people who absolutely had to have it.)

Owners-to-be would have to come back to pick up their pups at twelve weeks, but at eight or nine weeks, they could look over the mass of furry babies and try to choose one. Which, I knew, was impossible. Ultimately, I chose which pup went with which person. But the owners-to-be had to come for me to do that.

We explain that for the first year at least, this is a partnership. Jokingly, although we really mean it, we say that I will be their mother-in-law and have the key to the front door. Realistically, I tell them that for the first year of development, I will guide them through the feeding, care, growth, problems. In other words, get the pup on his feet, past the often turbulent, terrifying, volatile early months when the puppy who began at a pound or a pound and a half explodes to a hundred pounds in as little as six or seven months. I promise them that I would always be available, that they would have long lists of do's and don'ts, endless emails, phone calls, warnings, shopping lists, and visits. And so people who wanted these pups came. They came from California, from Oklahoma, from Florida, Texas, New England, New York, and from nearby.

The pups are not cheap. They are, I think, the most expensive of Newfoundland puppies. So my first question to inquiries was, "Do you have disposable income?" The initial payment is nothing compared to the possible collateral damage down the line. I want these people to be able to care for this dog no matter what goes wrong. Love, honor, and obey. In sickness and in health. Which adds up. Please, I beg them, get pet insurance.

One couple decided a pup was their lost dog reincarnated because he lifted his paw to them. Most pups do this, but that's what the prospective parents felt and I wasn't about to argue. Some wanted the perfect show dog. The owner and his trainer-to-be sat in the office for hours "going over" the puppies, watching them move, standing them on a grooming table to see their confirmation, how straight their legs were, the layback of the shoulders, the drop of the ears, (Ears should come just to the nose), the measurement between the elbow and the shoulder and the shoulder to the center of the back (Should be equal). There is measurement and then there is the aesthetic. I don't measure. I squeeze my eyes and predict. Some wanted dogs who looked like the ones they'd lost. Some wanted dogs who did not at all remind them of dead dogs. Some didn't want a puppy at all, or at least the wife didn't.

Bob decided one family was an absolutely bad, even terrible choice, but they returned and returned. The husband was trying desperately to convince his wife. The wife who had never had so much as a goldfish, worked on Wall Street all day; we wondered if she had white leather furniture. (She didn't. We visited them a year later.) The husband, who had a friend with two Newfies, decided he had to have at least one. He had fallen in love. His wife was not easy to convince. She was petite and neat, no match for a dog who would weigh fifty pounds more than she and tower above her when he wanted to kiss her face. Hubby worked hard to convince her, kept bringing her back. Then he read our five page single line contract which was more how-to than legal, and actually rewrote every word in it. Bob continued to have a bad feeling about this couple, but I was totally charmed by him, his intelligence, his deep respect for his wife's needs, and his utterly unbridled and compulsive editing. But litigious he might very well be. I also liked the wife very much. I knew she was trying because she knew her husband really wanted a buddy. I explained, after having gone over what situation the dog would be in and warned that leaving a Newfy alone during the day was the utmost cruelty – a small death; I told him he had to take the dog to work every day, crate him in his office and walk him or get an employee to exercise him. Turns out he had sixty-five employees but he would walk the dog himself. Unfortunately his landlord didn't want dogs. So prospective owner turned in his BMW, bought a van for the dog, moved his offices, put in an expensive fence, and called me to ask why I didn't want to sell him a puppy. I said, "Because you will sue me if he gets so much as a flea." He laughed and signed the original unedited contract and I gave him one of the best puppies in the litter. The couple turned out to be the most wonderful, attentive, loving of owners.

We've made some painful errors in judgment. The very slick divorce attorney who came from California, signed both copies of the contracts, his and ours, then took both contracts away with him, his and ours, and having agreed not to neuter the dog until he was full grown (for health reasons), gave him a great name (Cowboy) neutered him anyway, at six months, let him swim in the deathly toxic Salton Sea which resulted in seizures, gave him up, Thank God, to a wonderful woman we found in California, who rescued the poor unloved dog, cured him of the seizures (which he's been without for five years now) and has him still on his feet at ten and a half.

This match-making, head-hunting, guess work, finding the right owners for the right dogs is a considerable challenge, makes your head itch. Bob and I argued a great deal about whom WE should choose, never mind how hard the prospective owners were trying to choose their puppy although I knew full well, ultimately, they would get the puppy I thought they should have.

There was one little girl who was very pushy -- Miss Orange, the one who had screamed at another puppy blocking her path when she was a week or so old. Miss Orange had learned at four weeks how to climb stairs, which was amazing. Intellectually, Miss Orange was way ahead of the other pups, daring, and willful. When the pups were allowed to go through their little doorway into the outside

161

run, they would invariably get stuck because they all wanted to go out at once. The door was plugged up. But not for Miss Orange. She leaped over them all. She would be a handful but a wonderful, intelligent girl with great hips and a lot of what we call "attitude". Attitude works in the show ring. Here I am. Look at me. Look at me. Aren't I terrific? She was. She went to a family who showed dogs, had trained their dogs, and had great expectations for her. Unfortunately she chased the family cats and the owner decided after a thousand emails and phone calls that if she spayed her, she wouldn't chase cats. I finally gave up arguing. There was certainly no convincing the owner otherwise.

Early spaying and neutering increases the chances of cancer and screws up the growth system and has nothing at all to do with chasing or not chasing cats. Often if you see a long, tall, thin Newfy who limps it's because removing the hormones before they are full-grown reduces the muscular growth which is necessary to support the skeletal system and you really get physical damage because there are not enough strong muscles to support the body mass. I finally gave up. The dog survived. The cats survived. We all survived. Unfortunately Miss Orange had the finest hips ever tested in a Newfoundland and it was a great pity to spay her. I should have kept her. She would have been a true benefit to the genetic pool. But it had become, after all, just too much work to convince the owner otherwise, and of course, she could spay her without my knowing just as well. The Newfoundland world is a small and gossip-driven world. Everyone knows each other. Breeders protect and support each other. I would have found out.

Now Bulldozer (Mr. Yellow) was a problem. I wanted him. I wanted him for his markings, his head, his great bone, and his superior size. He was certainly the biggest boy in the litter. But I didn't think I would be able to handle him. I astonished a family who would have taken any one of the males by offering him Bulldozer -- the pick of the litter. From

162

day one, I had chosen Mr. Dark Blue but I moved away from my initial choice because Bulldozer was so impressive: a keeper. I didn't think I could handle Bulldozer and, because there would be constant food altercations in my kennel, I shifted back to Mr. Dark Blue (Ben). Bulldozer went out to a great family. I was so not smart but lucky. To everyone's surprise, Mr. Dark Blue ended up twenty pounds heavier than Bulldozer. Both boys have lived happily ever after. Ben is a champion and a successful stud, and is in my backyard. Bulldozer found his place in another backyard and on the sofa. He didn't like showing because it meant leaving his family and that wasn't in his nature.

A woman from the Far West wanted two of my best puppies for showing. As a young woman she had lived at the Waldorf while she studied voice in NYC for two years and I could only assume her good fortune and fortune probably continued into later life. She was a consummate shopper and very demanding. She called daily to make sure she was getting the two best puppies. When I explained and explained that I keep the best for myself, she grew even more demanding, called more often. She had shown horses, knew the routine, obviously still had disposable income as showing is expensive, lived in the blizzard boonies in the Midwest, couldn't possibly drive here, promised to drive here as I wouldn't ship, kept calling and demanding the best, the very best. Against my better judgment and because show homes are hard to find, and because the woman's phone calls had worn me out, and because she continued to be unable to drive because of the blizzards, her husband's back surgery etc. etc., I finally agreed to fly the puppies. It would be easier on them to fly together. Growing up together would be a gift to them. I sent her a male and female. Although I realized later that she was either lying or fooling herself or both, she decided she didn't want the male because he had seven (we counted) white hairs on his black body and couldn't possibly be shown (totally wrong) and she sent the poor little thing back across country. A perfect three month old gentleman, he came out of his cage – his clean cage after hours and hours of flying, transfer, and flying again -- wagging his tail in Newark, happy to be back with us and is in a home nearby where they don't mind the seven white hairs. The truth probably was the woman couldn't handle two puppies and it seemed, from what I could gather and imagine, couldn't handle her disapproving husband or two puppies.

People made demands, changed their minds: a male, oops, maybe a female, a show dog, a pet, a breeding dog, a little one, a really big male, a white face, a small female, a husband, a best friend. Everyone came in with a laundry list until a pup would look at them, make eye contact, lick their faces, and the laundry list was forgotten. What everyone really wanted was something utterly beautiful to love them. My puppies were ready to love, needed love, and we certainly couldn't give them enough. People who had been here once to see the pups, Elsa, Solomon and all the relatives, returned for their pups. I had sent them reams of emails and insisted they read a how-to-raise a puppy book. Some drove across country. Some flew. Two people from Los Angeles came out and flew back with four, two of them for other people who had already been here.

There's something magical about people meeting their pups. I usually bring the pup I'd chosen for them to the front door and pass it to them. I cry. They cry. They fall in love. That's their puppy. I know of many breeders who will wash the puppy they want the owners to choose, fluff him up so he looks larger than the rest. I didn't have the time. Once the pup is in the owner's arms, although they look around carefully at the others, my decision has been fortified. Actually the pups in Elsa's litter looked so much alike, it was fairly simple for everyone to make the decision, my input being far more informed than anyone else's out of sheer experience and a squint-eyed aesthetic. I can see who they will be.

Now and then a pup chooses its owner. I've seen it. It's happened to me, which is how I ended up with Solomon, the father of Elsa's puppies. When I stood nearby, everyone in Solomon's whelping box was busy; they glanced at me to see if I had food, then ignored me. The pup I had chosen because of his coloring and his head ignored me. But Solomon would not take his eyes off me. He knew he was to be my puppy. Whenever he made eye contact with me, I knew he was trying to tell me something. He wanted to stay. I was his IT. He was correct. He just had to convince me and he worked at it, running up to the gate when he heard me, barking at me, kissing me when I picked him up.

One little girl, who became Coco and was to go to Chicago, chose her owner. The day Coco's family-to-be arrived, all the pups were in an outdoor paddock, crowding at the gate to see who was in the car. Coco, who had shown herself as shy and non-confrontational, was suddenly alert as the young woman who was to be her mom approached the gate. Coco demonstrated activity totally unlike any I'd ever seen from her. She rushed the sixteen, leaped over them, slammed her way to the gate, found her place at the front of the gate, and said to her mom. "I'm here. I'm right here. I've been waiting for you." That was it. Although hubby, in-laws, two other visitors, and myself were standing there, Coco ran right to her mom and they've never been apart since. I had decided Coco would be a good match already but it was Coco who really decided. It was a remarkable heart-breakingly beautiful performance. Everyone cried at the sweetness and the magic. How did Coco know? It was the same way Solomon knew that he was to be the chosen one. I think, in fact, I am quite certain, these dogs, even these puppies, know more about us than we will ever know about them.

Most of the owners have made email connections with each other. I send emails out very often. Do this; don't forget that. Read this article? Remember two pounds gain a week, no more. I have heard from one gutsy owner that

165

everyone is afraid of me. I considered this for a while, felt terrible that I had somehow failed. Then, *then*, I felt good. As long as you take good care of my babies, whatever you think about me, is okay. But you better listen up. The kind of owner I like the most is the neurotic owner, the paranoid owner, the one who calls me every other day.

When breeders get together we are like old women sitting around the pool in Miami Beach bragging about how well our sons and daughters married. Cowboy, not only no longer has seizures, he has a good view of the ocean, his own pool, a private golf course, a beyond belief back yard for California, a vacation home in the woods, a mom who cooks for him, and a career as a well-loved therapy dog, as well as two other Newfies to play with. Three of mine live together and go on a month long road trip every summer. And these two live in three houses: farm, beach, and Manhattan mansion. And how about the philanthropist/model who takes her boy everywhere she goes? And this one flew to LA with a VIP escort, first class, goes to work every day, meets famous people, and eats kosher food, a bite for you, a bite for me. These two work in a pet store as greeters, have two kids to play with, live on the bay, and hang out in boats. These two do ocean rescue in France. These belong to hockey stars and fly around in private planes. These…and so on. I've gone to visit many of the pups, lived their lives for a few days, approved whole-heartedly. Well, some not so, but if the dog is clean and happy, in good physical shape, and outgoing, we all feel very lucky with our owners. On the other hand, the wealthiest people I ever sold a puppy to had a devastating experience. As we did also when we arrived on a planned visit and were met only by their house man. This young dog limped over to us, sniffed us, growled at us, and a few weeks later died of heat stroke as someone on staff hadn't paid attention and let him out with the dog walker for two and a half hours in Central Park on one of the hottest days in NYC. They were devastated. The dog had received plenty of attention and all the care in the world, but not from the people he needed the most. When you have taken every breath with these babies, disasters like this kill us. Owners and breeders suffer alike. It isn't easy to let a puppy go no matter how wonderful a home they are going to. Sometimes, if I have one of those intuitive inklings, I call Mary Long up to find out how the pup *is really* doing. I once took a ten month old male back who was intended for show. The owner felt he "hadn't turned out". The horror was she had not yet given him a name. That was a judgment error on my part. Many breeders have long applications. I don't because "wanters" can be pretty savvy. I just have to know the people, trust in my own judgment, which has admittedly failed me now and then. I talk to their vets, their past breeders, anyone who can give me support or info. Ultimately I have to trust that the owners will fall in love and dedicate themselves, heart and soul, to their dog as a friend, who will not be simply another acquisition.

CHAPTER TWENTY ONE

The pups simply could not all disappear overnight. One by one, two by two each time. Even though Elsa had distanced herself from them, she would have been crazed, I'm sure. It wasn't that she didn't have motherly feelings for them. She knew they were hers. She often ran in to check on them, ran out just as fast, but checking on them nevertheless. They would jump her, climb her, nail her nipples. Horrified, she would race to leave, knocking over the shaky contraptions that contained them. And they would chase her until we corralled them. Poor Elsa. Her dual natures were in conflict with each other. As we let a few go, Elsa seemed alright. But each time *my* heart broke. I convinced myself I was protecting Elsa. I was also protecting myself. Will these people do everything right? Trusting the universe was easy. Trusting these people was quite another. I was more fearful than sad. I was happy they would have loving attention, a real home, their own mommy. But so many people buy dogs as they buy lamps, with the same level of commitment. Turn it on when you want it. Once the puppy arrives it's adorable. Then it's a problem and no longer cute. The first few weeks were busy with phone calls, in and out. What is she eating? Are you crating her? You have to crate her to toilet train. You didn't read the how-to book yet? Page 15, house training. What does she weigh? Is she sleeping near you? Did you get the carpets down? Are you changing the water often? Not because it's empty, but because they know when it's stagnant. Mine race to drink from the toilet if they hear a flush. They need fresh water at all times. What about their vitamins? Every day? Are they in a puppy class yet? Have you kept the shot schedule up to date?

Some folks were difficult. Some were wonderful. Some had negative, defensive answers for every suggestion. Some reassured me too much. There had been the doubters, the men who didn't want to listen to a woman, the women who listened only to their husbands, the husbands who listened only to vets, certainly not women.

The engineer from the south was one of the latter. I think feminism has taken a long time to sink southward. He and his wife were a pleasant, handsome, sincere, educated couple. She was a nurse, therefore a natural and experienced caretaker. They were kindly people without children, ready to indulge their new puppy child. Too much. Their vet told them to keep the pup on puppy food until he was a year old. I had told them to put him on adult food because otherwise he would grow too fast. When a giant dog grows too fast so much cartilage is produced it doesn't have time to turn into bone. The bits of cartilage break loose, rot away, and self - destruct which was exactly what my poor beautiful innocent puppy did while his loving and truly devoted owners kept feeding him rich puppy food and he, crippled and broken, had to be put down before he was a year old. I had pleaded with the engineer. But because I wasn't a scientist, he said, and had published no papers and his venerable vet (unlike my vet and every other breeder I knew) said keep him on puppy food, he kept the poor baby on puppy food. Wouldn't budge. I considered picking him up. I didn't. This was many litters before Elsa's, and litters before I became savvy myself.

Meaning well is just not enough. That puppy was endangered. The owners were devastated. They meant well. Other people just tossed their money and time into the toilet. Years ago one puppy, I was told after the fact, was itching. The owner took him to a vet and had hundreds of dollars' worth of allergy tests, antibiotics, special sprays, lots of medicated baths, everything the vet suggested, then, and only then, the owner called me. The dog was still itching. What should she do? What, I asked, politely, is he eating? "Just his food with salmon treats:" "Oh," I said patiently, "if you had only told me he was itching before putting him through that regime. His uncle is allergic to fish." Breeders know more than vets about their line, about their breeds. We tell each other the news long before it gets into the textbooks. It takes great energy and patience to train the vets. Not that we don't use them constantly but there are issues and protocols we've had to come up with fast long before the information becomes canonized and trickles down to the vets. Breeders constantly share information with each other and with their owners. When a prospective buyer calls and can't remember the name of the breeder he bought his last Newfoundland from, he goes off the list.

For these reasons and many, many more the latest contract has all the directions and watch-out-fors, don't-ever-do's, right inside, above where the new owners have to sign. Now, after our own painful experiences, the directions on feeding are part and parcel of the contract which they have to read sitting with us, which they have to sign, which they have to agree to under penalties of large fines. They have to feed what I feed and how much I feed and weigh in every two weeks and gain no more than two pounds a week or else. We've learned so much all in an agonized effort to protect these puppies from danger. Much of me wants to run down the driveway after them. "Wait, wait. I'm coming too." How do you walk away from that pain of a dog whose cartilage breaks down? Of a dog who is run over? Of a dog who suffers? The dog who dies of heat stroke after an hour running on the hottest day in the city? A three month old puppy goes out on the boat. The engine turns on, terrifies her. She jumps into the harbor. That stupidity? How do you forgive? You go on and learn.

But then there are the others, physicians, men, who listen, who help, who research, who send medicines, articles, who teach me, as well as people who hit the web, worry, learn, and most of all share. This one knows all about food. This one knows a lot about behavior and training. This one knows a good product to clean up carpets. This one discovered a great product for a hotspot, a new toy, a new training trick, a garden hose without phthalates in it. At last, thanks to the emails, we have a wonderful support system even when I'm not around to answer the phone or just don't know the answers.

CHAPTER TWENTY TWO

A Long Essay on Dog Persons and Person Dogs

Twenty years ago when my daughter Jill married we used three of our dogs as her wedding party. The first Molly was Matron of Honor, the first Ben and Toby were Best Men and Ring Bearers as they pulled an antique goat cart with the pillow on which the ring lay. The newspaper refused to publish the wedding announcement, not believing it. No one else at that time was using dogs in their wedding ceremony and the society editor refused to believe that we had. Now having the family dog participate has become common. We had to wait until the judge who performed the ceremony returned from a vacation and testified to the newspaper that we had indeed used our dogs. A guest at the wedding whom I didn't know and who didn't know me approached and opened a conversation by asking, "Do you believe these people are selling this gorgeous home to get a better place for their *dogs?*" I had to answer, "Yes, I believe it."

He smiled politely and moved on. I was a kook, a dog person. I am not alone. Now many people proudly identify their madness. "I am a dog person. "The phrase has become part of the language. More and more sophisticated people say to me, "You know, I'm a dog person." Oh, I understand immediately. They feel as I feel. Increasingly nowadays, when a person is described as a dog person, a set of values and behaviors is understood, the wildest acceptable and forgiven. "Oh, well, she's a dog person." The phrase has magnetized meaning. Dog person. Soon we'll be putting a dash between the word dog and the word person and someday it just might become one word, something like 'pocketbook' or 'highway' or 'armchair'. When you say I'm a dog person, it doesn't mean merely that you like dogs or have a dog. It means that you are moving over, that you are a new hybrid, a new person, remaining yourself but also moving into the world of dogs, a new partnership, behind the lattice work. Dog persons are remaking themselves to include the dog image just as the dogs model themselves after their humans: to become like humans, to move into their place in the partnership, neither servant nor master, but a marriage, a deep and abiding relationship. We persons become more than persons. And our dogs become more than just dogs. We both break down the boundaries between us. I remind myself of Elsa "making believe" that she's speaking. She would sit in the center of a circle of humans having a conversation, studying their faces as she searched for meaning, listening to their words, moving her lips, making believe that she too was speaking, or perhaps mirroring in order to learn how to speak, going through the motions, trying with everything she knew to break down the boundaries between us. Just as I do.

I want to think that many animals try to break down the boundaries and I don't think it's only about food. On safari in Africa, I was sitting in the lodge at the Amboseli Game Park, sitting in the dark because, suddenly, in that wilderness, the power had gone out. People with guns ran out into an area not far from the lodge. Later, it was explained to us that it was always the same elephant who knocks out the electric fence. "Every time. She's just trying to get in." Me too. The lights came back on. The elephant remained out there in that vast darkness and my heart went out to her. I wished I could have gone to her, touched her, talked softly to her. She's just trying to get in. I know the feeling. I've been trying to get in since I was a little girl. I'd been on the wrong side of the lattice work long enough.

What is a dog person? A dog person is also just trying to get in, into the sweet and comfortable world of dogs. Dog persons seem kinder. We have empathy for our

173

dogs, try to understand them, not simply give them commands and treat them as subservient creatures or amusements. Dogs are wonderfully Other, Alien, but willing to be us. We are Other and willing to be them. They are not lesser creatures. Dog persons see dogs and feel dogs as Other, not as animals. We often have to remind ourselves that the creature sitting at our feet is an animal. Dog persons seem to have let go of controlling the universe. They trust it more. Also, they have dogs to guide them through, to connect them to a greater universe, to nature. When I was a visiting professor at a large university, no one on the faculty greeted me as we passed each other in my department offices. I don't know if they were worried I would take their jobs, their students, or I was too fat, too old, or dressed oddly. I don't know what they were thinking but it was very uncomfortable and unfriendly. Until one day I brought my dog to school. Then, dog on leash, I met a lot of colleagues. They stopped to chat with me. I'd been there for months and had never had a word. Had I become more trustworthy? More human? The boundaries are dropped between human and dog, and then just so lightly, with much less trust, between human and human.

Dog persons seem messier. Houses grow messier; clothes hairier and slimier, cars a disaster. The dogs are groomed better now than their owners. We let go, accept the world as it is, as we are. Why do we let go of the universe? Because, as our dogs, we are now more comfortable in the way the world is. We don't have to change it, control it. That's what we've learned from them. Accept, trust. So if the muddy dog gets on the leather couch to sit next to us, what's more important? And if the desecrated leather sofas have become the storage unit/burial ground for the remains of peanut butter sandwiches and or other purloined greasy goodies, so be it. The jewel-toned velvet throw pillows stand in luminescent testimony to the silvery trails of saliva of our sofa grave-robbers. Our home is a dog home. So be it.

174

Although I'm still not sure what a dog person is but I know I've become one and I am very much not alone.

I've always loved the story of a Newfy playing hide and go seek with two children. The children hid and she had to find them. And of course she would. One day, however, they couldn't find her. At last they heard a soft woof behind the shower curtain. She had learned not only to hide but whisper. Of course she knew how to hide as a dog but now she was hiding as a person. Defining herself as them. It's my turn to be you. My dogs bring us toys because they want to play, bring us shoes because they want to go outside, signal us any way they can. Sure they learn sounds and connect them to actions that they must do -- that's training. But they also concoct actions to tell *us* things. And we barely listen. They understand us far better than we understand them.

When a psychologist brought an infant chimp into his home to grow up with his new baby, that chimp thought she was a person also. And why not? One of her games was to sort through a pile of photographs and separate the animals from the people. She did this perfectly until it came to a photo of herself which she carefully put in the pile of people photographs. Are these animals so mistaken? Is it a joke when Elsa sits in a chair, rides in a car, gets an ice-cream cone, goes to McDonalds, sleeps in my bed? Is this an evolution? A transition? Are our dogs getting ready for something...for a big change? Ishtar once told Mary Long the animal communicator. "There is one thing, if we did that, it would blow their minds." I don't know what that thing is. I assume that's a promise of language. Or perhaps they're getting to walk around on two legs or play the piano? Or teach us telepathy? Animals think, feel, act, change. The ones who can adapt, certainly the dogs, adapt to what we are and, of course, vice versa. We adapt to them.

When the new owners came to see their eight week old pups, Solomon and Elsa were also invited to be there—to visit and perhaps to interview. They would make their judgments. Is this person dangerous, trouble, unsteady? If one of them growled (unthinkable) or backed away, or even hid, or in some way showed avoidance, it would mean to me those people were unworthy of puppies, I would have taken my dog's reading seriously. Having studied them and judged humans from almost the day they were born, they understand people. Solomon stopped as many people as he could, sat before them, put his paw on their shoulders, and looked into their eyes. If he had cigars, I think he would have handed them out. Elsa came up, pretty with a new pink bib around her neck which read, DO YOU THINK THIS MAKES ME FAT? We were making fun of her but she was very serious about her responsibility as a hostess. She went to work immediately, leaned against everyone, greeting them, stared into their eyes, a penetrating stare. "Why is she looking at me this way?" the person she focused on would ask, uncomfortably. They didn't understand dogs. A bad sign. Not quite a personality defect but something that deserved watching.

If Elsa isn't a person, she certainly behaves like one. Is it too much to say, if they behave like people, it would follow that they think like people? Or they think like dogs because dogs are becoming people as well. Dog R Us? Are we looking at evolution overwhelming instinct? The anecdote I've used again and again to explain Newfies to people is about the Newfy puppy and the Rottie puppy who were raised together. They sat on their Toronto porch and watched every day as the newspaper boy came by on his bicycle and tossed a paper on the porch. But one morning, at newspaper delivery time, about the time they were coming into their ten month old male hormones, the Rottie jumped the boy, knocked him off his bicycle, held him by the throat. The Newfy leaped from the porch and killed the Rottie. What were you thinking, Newfy? Who do you think you really are? What do you think you are? Are you us? You are, aren't you?

Elsa and her pups had been in trouble because Elsa had shifted over too much. She had become too human. Her instincts were atrophied by what she'd learned from us. We don't clean tushies; we don't eat waste. Only dogs do that.

Every once in a while I am astonished, reminded, that my dogs are actually dogs. They are more than that for me. Their presence is so like the presence of a human, a sister, a lover, a close, close friend, a mother, a daughter. I forget they are animals. In fact, I would argue that they are something beyond, a delicate combination of us and them, a combination they've agreed to and worked toward for thousands of years. I've observed them too long to doubt that. They know what's going on. Often non-locally.

Reggie, a four year old from one of my litters, lives with and lives for two children. Reggie was out for a walk on lead two blocks from his home when his little girl who had stayed home hurt her toe. Reggie broke loose, bolted home. People were treating the toe with ice cubes. Reggie pulled his cool collar ice-filled necklace from the freezer as well and brought it over to his little girl. He knew exactly what was happening. I was returning from a dog show once. I came home to find my husband out on the ice with a broken shoulder, unable to lift himself up. A six month old puppy, Laalaa, now grandmother of Elsa's litter, was up on the hill above him barking and barking, calling for help. And a big male lay next to my husband for a long time, watching over him, protecting him, keeping him warm. No, these dogs aren't human, but they are certainly more than dogs. And Katie, who is Elsa's grandmother, woke me up one night to let me know that there was an electrical fire in the basement, saving all of our lives. She woke me up. I thought she wanted to go outside to relieve herself. No, she led me, not to the front door, but to the basement. When the danger was over, we sat with the firemen on a bench outside the house. Katie went to each of the firemen, leaned against their legs, and looked up earnestly into their faces. I knew she was thanking them. Years ago when hundreds of elk were being allowed to die of starvation at Yosemite, the director of something or other at the Federal level announced that the elk were not suffering because they had no feelings. I wanted to thrust a stake through his cold heart. My dogs have feelings. Recently I watched a You Tube video of a dog running into traffic to rescue another dog who had been hit by a car, to watch her drag the injured dog out of the road, to safety. Their feelings may not be like mine but they are recognizable, familiar, and real.

Even though Elsa doesn't communicate noises with us, just with her echo friend and the coyotes, she tells us everything with her eyes and her body language. She demonstrated one remarkable day a basic genetic response that I know was deep and anciently embedded in the dog and human histories. Is this how it happened so long ago? Is this how we became friends? She and I had gone to visit a human friend. We were chatting in the front yard. A neighbor asked if she could bring her children over to see the big dog. As the toddlers approached, Elsa immediately dropped to the ground, flattened out, and crawled on her belly toward the babies. "Don't be afraid. I won't hurt you." Kindness. Elsa was kind to human beings, especially little ones who might need help. Maybe the dog/human friendship began with children. Kindness was in her DNA. A year old puppy girl in California, walking with her owner, saw a bear. She stood on her hind feet to make herself look large. The bear left. Judgment, kindness, bravery. I can be small. I can be big. Whatever my humans need.

I was walking on an ice-covered lake, at the edge. My first dog Ben dragged me furiously back by my coat sleeve. At my last step, the ice broke under my feet. He knew. What kind of innate action is this? I think of Katie thanking the firemen, leaning against their legs, looking into their eyes. Katie's daughter, Laalaa, as a service dog, was allowed into an emergency room with me once when I had a severe nosebleed. She knew exactly what was going on. Laalaa walked next to the wheelchair, watched and sniffed as I sat on the gurney, then methodically pressed against each and every person in the room and looked into their eyes. "I trust you," she was saying. "We are your friends. Take good care of Rhoda." Now she assured herself they would. Or, given Laalaa's powerful personality, they had better.

And these little puppies who are getting ready to take on their new work of taking care of us? They will be person-dogs and make dog-persons of their new owners. That's the Great Work. They'll guide us through the lattice work into the universe. They've been working on it for thousands of years. It's in their blood now. Imagine, just imagine what it means that it is *instinctive* for Newfoundlands to save people. Imagine. Instinctive. How long have they been with us? When are they going to really start talking with us?

When Ishtar, ancestress of them all, told Mary Long that Newfoundlands came from the star Sirius, came down to help us, were very small, close to the ground and if we wanted to know more we should check out the star, I so wanted to believe all of that, that they are more than dogs. Not easy. But I can at least believe they are here to help us. Buddha-like, they say, "I am here. How can I help you?" And yet when I hear them singing with the coyotes at night I wonder who else they are. Of course, I spend plenty of twilight zone evenings wondering who else I am, and as Elsa does, wondering who else I might become.

CHAPTER TWENTY THREE

Winter broke. The ground was still frozen but the snow was gone. Because there had been so little time and energy, I had ignored my grown dogs. But the sky was blue; the air was fresh, freezing, and I had missed my ladies terribly. So Laalaa, Katie, Elsa (grandmother, mother, daughter) and I went for a walk. Just as we passed the barn, there, at last, was the fox, or a fox, perhaps the one we called Vicky, sitting at the rise, in full sight, looking directly at me. My ladies were moseying about in the brush, far behind me. No one had ever reported a fox playing with or interested in my females, only with Solomon. But there she or he was, waiting? A sentinel? A greeter? A rabid fox about to attack me? I, in the big raccoon coat, smelling a bit like puppies and mother's milk, enveloped in my intimacies with Elsa and the pups, stopped. This time I didn't run nor did I hustle the ladies back to their kennel. I just stood still. The fox swung her/his head around behind him, looked back at me. Directing my attention? A message? Judging me? Recognizing me? What was behind him? Was he showing me something? Was it a him or a her?

Him. In the open area where the path to the creek and the path to the woods intersect another larger fox stood. The female. Vicky? And at her feet, three beautiful kits tumbling and chasing just as my puppies. A family. They too had babies. Was Sly the father? Had he returned or was this a new Sly? Was he showing me his family? It's easy to assume Sly was guarding his family. That would be the most natural assumption. If I have fox family organization correct, it was a male looking at me and behind him, with the kits, a larger fox: the female. Vicky or another Vicky. This is no way to guard your family, Fox. There are hundreds of wild acres here. They would be far safer away from us. My ladies were coming closer. I bent to hold onto their collars and, in the moment I did, a flash of white tail, tails. Sly, sentinel, protector, father, friend, turned away from us, and he and his little family were off, their arrogant fancy rears prancing up the trail into the deep woods. I would like to think Sly or perhaps Vicky had been saying to me, "See *our* puppies? We have babies too." I went back to the house, found a carton of eggs, and planted them one by one in the weeds where the foxes had just been. Maybe Sly and Vicky let me under the lattice work because I'd paid my dues with my puppies. Maybe, just maybe, they had recognized me. That one's alright. Whatever their reason, I knew I had been, for that brief moment, acceptable. It is not too much to believe that the fox was really presenting his babies to me? That the fox had invited me under the lattice work, finally. I had become, after all, a dog- person. That one's alright.

And Elsa? A year after her huge litter, Elsa bred again with Solomon and produced a single puppy. At last she was able to love without fear. She could be a dog. Her pup, a little male, slept next to her. She allowed him to nurse without pause; she cleaned him, cuddled him. Although we still watched him 24 hours in the beginning, she truly became his mother. At last, she fulfilled both selves. She is a lady and a dog. No more hiding under the cellar steps. We were both, Elsa and myself, on our way to become the Other.

A BRIEF EPILOGUE ABOUT WHY DOGS BARK

Wolves don't bark. Coyotes yip, howl, scream, but they don't bark. Foxes screech. Elsa barks. Her half sister Bumper sings: "woo woo woo." If dogs descend from wolves who don't bark, how is it that dogs bark? Where did they learn to bark? From us?

At a Newfoundland Nationals in Wisconsin, on a clear cool night, a thousand or so Newfies, many of them sleeping outdoors in crates while their owners camped next to them, the Newfies started calling to each other. They didn't bark in a mass of noise. Each took a turn. I lay in my bed laughing as one after the other picked up the conversation, passed it on. "We are table number one. Where is table number two?" I wanted to throw on my jacket and go outside to bark with them. "I'm here. Over here." The call went from one to the other for hours, locating each other, not a melee of barking but a great, grand reunion of Newfy Nation.

Crazy as it may seem, I would like to think the barking is the way my dogs were trying to speak, to communicate the way humans do: to make our sounds. The thousand Newfies were sharing the sheer pleasure of being together I think of Elsa sitting among a group of people and moving her lips, joining the conversation, mimicking us, making believe she was talking, working at it at any rate. How did it all begin? Now, in human time, the bark has become the dogs' genetic feature, a fixture, as fixed as their innate willingness to work for us, learn from us, mirror us, and, most of all, take care of us --all these gifts learned and encoded so long ago when our world was young and we shared our beginnings with the dogs.

In the book The Singing Neanderthal (Steven Mithen, Harvard University Press, October, 2007) I read an amazing fact: many autistic people ... a greater percentage than the general population ... have perfect pitch. Many of them are musically adept, some even savants. It is as if not having language, an innate musical ability has blossomed. It is as if music were an original sound. Remember when Gabby Giffords was recovering from brain injury? The doctors had her singing. Music is another part of the brain, an earlier part of the brain, often buried by the weight of language. In much the same way donkeys who worked in dark mines grew blind because they didn't use their eyes, using language to communicate atrophied our musical ability to communicate. Use it or lose it. Steven Mithen's theory surrounding this astonishing fact is that Neanderthals may have had a musical, emotional form of communication that was very different than language. It may be what happened when we Cro-Magnons moved in on them, talking, teaching, advancing with facts, real information that could be remembered and passed on to future generations. That so many autistic people have perfect pitch and that many of them are fine musicians is, to me, a stunning and far-reaching clue to our dogs' development. What that means in terms of my dogs is really stretching it.

But then I do stretch it. Lying there in the whelping room hour after hour I listened to my dogs howl with the coyotes, bark at each other, bark at us. I heard the fox screech. I heard Bumper sing her joyous woo woo woo's, starting with a low note and singing higher and higher up the octave depending on her mood. We always laugh, not at her, but for her because she's so happy to see us.

Wolves don't bark. Why do dogs bark? Wolves and coyotes howl. And dogs recognize the howl. My dogs wake up in the dead of night and howl back, responsively to the coyotes across the pond. They answer, repeating what the coyotes call out, call out in a primitive language that my civilized dogs remember deep in their genes. Dogs howl at sirens, fire engines, and coyotes. Dogs came from wolves. If wolves don't bark, where did dogs learn to bark? I think Bumper's woo woo woo's are left-overs from ancient times, that they originated before barking, when we sang without language. Is that what's lurking in Bumper's singing genes? Perhaps early dogs, always our companions, mimicked the singing Neanderthals. And perhaps barking originated with our primeval relationship with dogs. Could it be that the time dogs stopped howling and began to bark was the time humans began to speak? Along came Cro-Magnons with their newfound language and their dogs followed, syllable by syllable. Crazy, I know. But they mimic our behaviors. Could they be mimicking our sounds so many years ago? The paleoarcheologists now claim real dogs, not wolves, have been with us for 22,000 years. The coyotes howl and yip. A howl from a wolf seems closer to the musical but nothing like Bumper's singing. The barks from the dogs are not musical. They are more like words, syllables, separate from each other, like speech.

When Bumper sings, a rarity in my dogs and most dogs, she is greeting us with a melodic woo woo woo, an accomplished greeting, always the same notes, but only on the occasion of greeting a human, never when greeting another dog. She barks at Theo when he eats from her bowl, at other dogs, in excitement when they bark at each other. But sings only to humans. Elsa does not sing. Nor does she bark *at* us. She does, however, bark at herself for hours. She barks at her echo. Her kennel faces the ten acre pond. Her voice echoes back to her over the water and she barks in three beats and four beats. She and her echo friend carry on for hours, practicing speech with her own watery feedback.

Where did barking come from that it is passed on now in the genes?

I think about Elsa sitting in the middle of a circle of adults talking to each other, swiveling her head to each person as that person speaks, moving her own lips as if she too were part of the conversation…is that how it all began? Is this where it is going?

I dare to think the barking is something learned, from us, a proto language, a beginning. I dare to think our dogs are learning to be us just as we are learning to be them. We close Elsa's story with a story about Moby, our year and a half old, one hundred fifty pound boy in Los Angeles. He is the King of Rodeo Drive and, because of his great size and beauty, a tourist attraction when he eats lunch with people friends al fresco or strolls into Bulgari, where, as well as the other ultra shops on Rodeo Drive, he is welcome. Moby lives with his owner Barbara, a single, successful woman. Moby has his own well-attended website. One night his owner had nieces and nephews sleeping over. Twenty year old Carla went to sleep in Barbara's bed. Where Moby sleeps! Moby found Carla in the bed. Oh, oh, something is wrong, wrong, wrong. There is another being in my bed. So he climbed on the bed, stood over the sleeping Carla, straddling her, and watched her to see if she were dangerous. When she did not wake up, he determined she was not a threat. He climbed off the bed, returned with two cookies, and laid them carefully on her chest. After all, when Barbara puts him to sleep, *he* gets two cookies, so that's what we do. We - as in humans. Moby may look very much like a dog but he's learning to think like a human.